The
RUNNER'S
CODE

The RUNNER'S CODE

The Unwritten Rules of Everyday Running

CHAS NEWKEY-BURDEN

BLOOMSBURY SPORT
LONDON · OXFORD · NEW YORK · NEW DELHI · SYDNEY

BLOOMSBURY SPORT
Bloomsbury Publishing Plc
50 Bedford Square, London, WC1B 3DP, UK
29 Earlsfort Terrace, Dublin 2, Ireland

BLOOMSBURY, BLOOMSBURY SPORT and the Diana logo are trademarks of
Bloomsbury Publishing Plc

First published in Great Britain 2021

Illustrations on p. 6 and p. 208 by Neil Stevens

All suggestions and material in this book are for information purposes only.
Since each individual's personal situation, health history and lifestyle differs you
should use discretion before proceeding to do any of the exercises or techniques
described. The author and publisher expressly disclaim any responsibility for any
adverse reactions or effects that may result from the use or interpretation of the
information contained within this book.

Bloomsbury Publishing Plc does not have any control over, or responsibility for, any
third-party websites referred to or in this book. All internet addresses given in this
book were correct at the time of going to press. The author and publisher regret
any inconvenience caused if addresses have changed or sites have ceased to exist,
but can accept no responsibility for any such changes

A catalogue record for this book is available from the British Library

Library of Congress Cataloguing-in-Publication data has been applied for

ISBN: HB: 978-1-4729-8959-8; epub: 978-1-4729-8957-4;
ePDF: 978-1-4729-8955-0

2 4 6 8 10 9 7 5 3 1

Typeset in 10/14.5 GriffithGothic by Deanta Global Publishing Services,
Chennai, India
Printed and bound in in Great Britain by CPI Group (UK) Ltd, Croydon CR0 4YY

To find out more about our authors and books visit www.bloomsbury.com
and sign up for our newsletters

You always encourage me to run and write better,
so this one is for you, Chris

A NOTE ON THE AUTHOR

Chas Newkey-Burden is a running fanatic who has run at hundreds of events including marathons, half-marathons and over 100 parkruns. He writes about running for *The Guardian, Daily Telegraph, Metro* and *The i*, and has contributed to *Runner's World* and *Men's Health*. He is the author of several books, including *Running: Cheaper Than Therapy* and *Get Lucky: Rituals, Habits and Superstitions of the Rich and Famous*.

CONTENTS

Introduction   9

Welcome to the Tribe   11
- How to start running   12
- Home truths   18

Kit   23
- Gearing up   23

How to be a Considerate Runner   33
- The runner at home   34
- The runner out and about   39
- Run with your conscience   62

Nutrition   68
- Eat right   68

Events   80
- Your pre-event checklist   81
- Dos and don'ts during the event   90
- How to finish   100

Clever Running   104
- Learn from the experts   104
- How to run with a dog   122
- How to run into old age   126

Health and Safety   130
  • Prevention is better than cure   131
  • To run or not to run?   135
  • How to run in the rain   143
  • How to run in the dark   147
  • How to run in the cold   152
  • How to run in the sun   152
  • Learn to identify common injuries   156
  • Simple injury-prevention methods   158

A Bit of Fun   164
  • The good, the bad and the ugly   165

It's All in the Head   184
  • Listen up   184
  • Tricks of the mind   191
  • Take in your surroundings   198

Run Happy   200

The A–Z of Running   201

Acknowledgements   206

INTRODUCTION

Running is so simple. You put one foot in front of the other, then the other foot in front of that one. You keep doing that, quite quickly, until you've had enough. What more needs to be said?

Quite a lot more needs to be said. From safety to clothing, nutrition to stretching, this is a curiously complicated and layered hobby. *The Runner's Code* explores the unwritten rules of everyday running and helps you make the right choices.

Let's be honest: runners are a curious bunch. We are the sort of people who forego a lie-in on a winter's morning in favour of huffing round a freezing park before sunrise, or who train all year for a run so long that it makes our nipples bleed.

We are eccentric characters who might inadvertently rub other people up the wrong way, if we remained unchecked by codes. Most of us are lovely people and running is a lovely pastime. What keeps it lovely are the hitherto unwritten codes that we are bound by. The better we understand those codes, the more we can keep to them.

This *Code* helps you deliver your best performance (coping with running in different weather), advice on clothing (how many miles a pair of trainers can last, and whether or not it's ever appropriate to run topless) and pavement etiquette (how to deal with dawdling pedestrians on a busy street).

What should you do if you get caught short on a run? What's the correct form when it comes to acknowledging other runners? And how many times can you ask colleagues for marathon sponsorship? You will discover the answer to these, and many other dashing dilemmas, in the pages ahead.

We will also hear the thoughts of a string of fascinating people, who will tell us what they love and hate about running. Broadcasters, running coaches and football stars join authors of running books and podcasters to spill their loves and pet peeves about running.

The hope is that this book will help you run better and more responsibly, as well as bringing a smile to your face, as we explore the joy and, at times, absurdity of why we run.

WELCOME TO THE TRIBE

When you first start running, you join a tribe to which people of all speeds, shapes and sizes are welcome. This is a special club – the only membership condition is a pair of trainers and a willingness to put one foot in front of another. Quickly.

However, it can also be a bit bewildering. Friends and colleagues who run will have plenty of advice for you but some of them will contradict one another. You'll also find that when some runners offer advice they'll actually just be showing off about their own achievements. Then, when you look online, there are yet more tips and suggestions.

A lot of that information is irrelevant to you at this stage. You don't want to be overwhelmed, so the trick is to get the advice that you need as a beginner. No more, no less.

The early days of any runner are make or break. The ones who start up the hobby with good advice tend to stick at it, often for the rest of their lives. The ones who don't get good advice sometimes decide that running isn't for them and they never try it again. So, the stakes couldn't be higher. Luckily, you've got the *Code* to guide you.

HOW TO START RUNNING

Sometimes you just want to get going, so here is our equivalent of those 'quick start' pages you get in product manuals. If you follow these guidelines it will make starting running so much easier for you.

Walk/run

A great way to get into the groove of running as a beginner is to combine jogging and walking. So, if you are just getting started, try jogging for 30 seconds, walking for 30 seconds and then jogging for 30 seconds. As you grow in confidence in the weeks ahead, you can tweak the ratio, increasing the jogging sections and decreasing the walking sections, until you are purely jogging.

It's OK to go slow

Just as new converts to a religion can be more zealous than those who were born into it, so new runners can be more concerned with 'rules' than those who have been at it for years. Although experienced runners think nothing of slowing down or even walking during their runs, newcomers are often absolutely terrified to do so, for fear it will make them look bad. Take it from the *Code*: there is nothing wrong with taking a breather.

Short runs are better than no runs

So you don't have the time or the motivation for that 5km (3-mile) run you had planned for today? Why not head out for just 1.5km (1 mile)? You can do the longer distances another day but in the meantime you've kept your body and mind ticking over.

Don't go out too often

Newbie runners often ask how often they should run. Sometimes they assume they are meant to run every day. But in the early days, you shouldn't be doing more than a maximum of four outings every seven days.

Build distance gradually

Enthusiasm will be one of your greatest friends as a runner, but too much of it is a fast track to failure, disappointment and injury. This is particularly true when you're a beginner: it's so easy to aim too high, fail, and then say: 'I knew running wasn't for me'.

I've witnessed this quite a few times. Someone I vaguely know on social media sends me a private message to tell me that they've entered a marathon and need tips because they're completely new to running and 'can't even run for a bus'. I ask them when the marathon is, hoping it's at least 12 months away. They say: 'Oh, in eight weeks.' Eight weeks to go from being unable to run for a bus to running a full marathon? Don't be like those people. There will be time to run long distances, in the meantime just build gradually. Beginners' training programmes or the Couch to 5K app will help you.

Don't run too fast

When I told someone I'd run a marathon, she asked me how long it took. When I said four hours, four minutes, she asked: 'So you actually sprinted for four hours and four minutes? Wow!' She was so impressed I was tempted to not correct her but I did. However, her funny question does show that some non-runners assume that every run is meant to be a full-pelt slog. This isn't the case. When you are starting up, always aim for a comfortable pace. One way of nailing this is to check whether you can comfortably hold a conversation as you run. If you can't, you're running too fast.

Find your best time of day to run

IF YOU DISCOVER the best time of day for you to go out running then it's more likely that you'll do it regularly. Ultimately, there is never a bad time to run but to help you find your sweet spot, here is your rundown of the positives and negatives of each time.

Morning

Pros:

1 Your body burns calories faster on an empty stomach, so morning mileage can mean you reach any weight goals more quickly.

2 A study found that morning exercise leads to better sleep quality than afternoon or evening exercise.

▶

3 A morning run gets your daily mileage out of the way early, leaving you free to face the rest of the day with your fitness task already achieved, rather than wasting time debating when, or whether, you'll squeeze it in.

4 Many scientists say that morning is the best time of day to boost muscle.

5 Most races and events are held in the morning, so it is very useful to be accustomed to morning running, rather than having to adjust on the big day.

Cons:

1 Lung function is poor in the early hours, so you may find breathing – and therefore running – considerably harder.

2 Your body temperature is low in the morning, so your muscles are stiff and you're more likely to pick up an injury.

3 It's usually colder around dawn.

4 In winter, the pavements are more slippery in the morning. Be careful!

5 The rest of the day can stretch long when you've already run several miles before breakfast. All day, whenever you look at the time you find yourself thinking: 'Sheesh, is that all?'

Afternoons

Pros:

1 Your body temperature is higher after lunch and experts say this higher temperature makes athletes perform better.

2 If you always run during your lunch hour at work, running will never eat into your family time, meaning your partner and children will be happy with you.

3 An early afternoon trot breaks up the day and allows you to take stock of what you've done so far and what you have left to do.

4 Some runners find it easier to motivate themselves to get out there once they've been up and about for some hours.

Cons:

1 To make it work, you have to either have an early or a late lunch; just scheduling your food around an afternoon run can be enough to make you give up on it.

2 You're either going to end up having two baths/showers in one day, or be a bit smelly for half the day. This is far from ideal.

3 Weather data shows it is more likely to be raining after lunch. Some enjoy a rainy run from time to time, but probably not all the time.

Evenings

Pros:

1 A run at dusk can be a pleasant and fitting way to shake off any of the stresses of your day.

2 Although some runners find it hard to sleep after an evening run, others really love getting into bed with their muscles tired, and that post-run glow still bright.

3 When it's dark, you get to wear a head torch, and you can imagine you're in a film.

4 Running in the wee small hours can be fun. Big parks or busy city centres can feel wonderfully surreal as you trot through them at 1 a.m. (But stay safe.)

Cons:

1 Motivation can be tricky – you put off the run all day and then, come evening, you just might not feel like it after a long day at the office.

▶

2   For much of the year, it's dark out there at night. This can be depressing.

3   Safety is an issue. You have to try harder to make sure drivers can see you and criminals might be lurking in the park. Many women feel safer running in pairs after dark.

4   It's very antisocial: you miss out on a chat with the family, after-work drinks and other social events.

GUEST FEATURE   *Lexie Williamson*

A thing I love about running   That moment about five minutes into the run when your clunky, awkward legs find their rhythm, your heart settles into a nice pace and the whole thing shifts from mechanical to mental. Whoever insists that settling the mind must be done seated stock still in Lotus pose should try running alone on a cold, crisp, sunny morning through the woods; it is, without doubt, a kind of moving meditation.

A thing I hate about running   The first five minutes of the run! (See 'A thing I love about running'...) When your legs are on strike, all you can hear is puffing and wheezing and you can't quite shake off memories of the warm duvet. Push through that, though, and you're winning.

Lexie Williamson is the author of Yoga for Runners.

Don't worry about small aches

It's perfectly natural and normal for your muscles to ache a little when you first start running. However, if the pain lingers for days, or if it begins to even hurt to walk, then get it checked out.

Don't be a 'hero'

If you're injured, don't run again until you've fully recovered. Just don't. You may think you're Rocky Balboa as you limp along, but you'll risk turning a five-day lay-off into a five-month lay-off – or worse.

Anxious about crowds at events? Ease in gently...

For the more introverted runners, the biggest challenge of a running event is not the miles they spend panting along, but the big crowds and the sense of occasion. If you're concerned about this, a good way of testing the waters is to go along to an event as a spectator, to get a taste of how it all works. Alternatively, many longer-distance running events have smaller runs tagged on to them – such as a 5km (3-mile) fun run on the same day as a half marathon. Joining the smaller version is a good way in.

HOME TRUTHS

Running wisdom doesn't need to be long-winded, like a marathon. Sometimes it's short and sweet, like a 100m dash. So from footwear to mood swings, here are quick and easy tips to get your blood pumping.

Not all trainers are created equal

While it's true that you can buy surprisingly cut-price footwear in those cramped discount sportswear stores, you will pay a huge price in the form of discomfort, lack of bounce and risk of injury. So, head to a running store, where experts can analyse your running gait. They will fit you with the perfect pair for you, and won't necessarily cost the earth.

Nobody cares

As you bask in the physical and emotional benefits of running you can become hellishly evangelical. However, don't chew the ears off your non-athletic friends in the pub, and resist the temptation to plaster details of your every workout across your social networks. (There will be more about this later.)

Enrolling for a race is hugely motivating

'I've got a busy day ahead.' 'My legs ache.' 'Maybe I'll wait until tomorrow.' It's so easy to dream up excuses not to get out there and run when you've no objective target to aim for. Book yourself in for a big 10K event and feel your motivation soar.

Gadgets help... But only a bit...

Roll on your leg-compression stockings and slip into your five-finger shoes, tying them with LED shoelaces. Strap on the heart rate monitor, the Nike fuel band and fire up the running app. Neck a beetroot juice shot, don your Oakley® sunglasses and climb into your hydration backpack. Or just recognise that no gadget can compete with good, honest dedication. You improve on the road, not in the shops.

...So keep a training log

Never mind fancy gadgets, simply keeping a note of your daily, weekly and then monthly mileage can be a great motivator.

Boredom kills you first

Once you start running longer distances, boredom can become as big an enemy to you as physical fatigue. So find a way to keep your mind happy. I found that once I'd loaded up my player with audiobooks and free podcasts, the miles just flew by.

GUEST FEATURE *Billy Wingrove*

A thing I love about running: The thing I love about running is the after-effect. You've released them endorphins and your mind and body feel more alive than ever. Getting out on a run improves both your mental and physical strength.

A thing I hate about running: What I don't like about running is how boring it is for me – lol! If I'm honest, I have never actually enjoyed running. I prefer to play sport to get fit but that being said, running is a part of my everyday life and I know I must maintain it for the health of my body and mind.

Billy Wingrove is one half of the enormously successful football freestylers, The F2. Follow him on IG: @billywingrove.

Mood swings

Runners' high is a thing – a lovely, glowing, life-enhancing thing. But so is runners' grump. If you've trained a bit too hard you can feel pumped up and worn out at the same time, and find yourself arguing with everyone. At such times, avoid irritating line managers at work and step away from that Facebook debate about politics.

Remember that the end justifies the means

Some runs will be great fun. Some runs will be a bit boring. But you will always, always, feel better for having done them.

Fanatics fail

If your body and your running schedule disagree, listen to your body. While it's easy to be all masochistic about running and feel that you must stick to your plans come what may, if one of your legs feels like it's about to fall off then you might want to rest it, rather than sticking to a plan you made weeks ago. Running schedules are guidelines, not religious rules to follow fanatically.

What if ...
a pedestrian won't get out of the way?

Sometimes you are running on a narrow path or a crowded pavement and you find yourself stuck behind a pedestrian. This can be very highly frustrating. If you are aiming to complete your run at a particular pace, or even if you have just reached a nice momentum and want to maintain it, it's annoying when someone won't let you pass.

But this isn't a time to try to win the argument or to get worked up about who is in the right. The roads are full of angry, territorial drivers. We don't need that sort of tension

---

on the pavements. Plus, there might be a good reason for the pedestrian's lack of co-operation. They may have a disability that prevents them from easily moving to one side, or they may not understand your request to get through.

So, rather than scaring or enraging others, just count to 10 and wait until the moment comes when you can pass safely. At the time, it can be annoying and you may want to remonstrate with them, but later, when you get home, you'll probably thank yourself for being patient.

KIT

Once upon a time, running kit was just any old clothing you could throw on. People would jog round their local park in jeans and everyday trainers or football boots. Where now people wear technical tops that wick the sweat away from them, people once ran in cotton T-shirts or rugby shirts, which became heavy and soaked with sweat.

It wasn't just amateurs who wore curious clobber. The legends did, too. Emil Zátopek, a Czech runner from the 1950s who won four Olympic gold medals, used to train wearing heavy combat boots. Then there was the Ethiopian runner Abebe Bikila, who won the 1960 Rome Olympic Marathon while running barefoot.

GEARING UP

Running gear is now a huge industry all of its own. We have come so far, haven't we? But that doesn't mean we don't still suffer wardrobe malfunctions. With running gear growing more and more specialist and trendy, and running gadgets becoming more intricate, getting the right stuff has become more of a minefield. So, in the pages ahead, the *Code* will walk you through what to wear, what not to wear and how to clothe yourself with dignity, for yourself and for the sake of others.

Always wear clean kit

Sometimes when you're getting ready for a run you realise you've forgotten to wash your kit. Well, you think, it wouldn't hurt to go out in some slightly smelly gear. It's all in the open air, after all. Actually, running in smelly kit does hurt, as anyone you run past will tell you. No one wants a waft of your days-old sweat, so just remember to wash your kit. This is doubly important if you will be running with others.

Dress for the temperature you'll be 10 minutes into a run

When the weather is mild, it's easy to decide what to wear for a run. But on particularly hot or cold days, it can be a trickier decision. The risk of over- or underdressing is huge.

Fortunately, a simple technique can make it easier for you: dress like it's warmer than it actually is because as you run, your core body temperature is going to increase. Or, to come at it from another angle, dress for the temperature you will be 10 minutes into the run.

If you feel very slightly cold as you stand outside stretching before you set off, you've probably got it right and will avoid the shivering annoyance of running with too little on, or sweltering your way through the race after overdressing. And don't get me started on the awkwardness of running with a jacket tied round your waist, constantly worrying it's going to slip off without you noticing.

Helen Croydon

A thing I love about running: The feeling of using my body. Feeling the little engine inside us ignite and traverse the land no matter what the terrain. We're so reliant on cars or other contraptions to get us anywhere in modern society that we forget what a marvel our own physiology is. Feeling your muscles work and the air go through your lungs is the antidote to our over-reliance on convenience.

A thing I hate about running: That first five minutes of a run in the winter when you're just wearing a thin running top. Five minutes is what I find it takes for my heart rate to rise and send the blood through me to warm up. You can always tell an amateur runner by the extra layer they have tied around their waists. They haven't learned yet that five minutes of being cold at the beginning is better than 25 minutes of being boiling if you wear too much.

Helen Croydon is the author of This Girl Ran.

Shop for running shoes in the afternoon

Your feet swell up as the day progresses. Given that your feet also swell up during a run (regardless of the time of day) it's best to try on shoes when your feet are a bit swollen.

Respect runners in non-running gear

Younger readers might like to make sure that they are sitting down for this section. Once upon a time, technical running gear didn't exist. A 'wick' was something in a candle and the colours for running clothes were gentle rather than radioactively garish.

So what did runners wear? Brace yourself for this: they once ran in cotton. Actually, some runners still do. At any running event, there will be a broad scale of modernity, or otherwise, among the gear worn by dashers. Some will be kitted out in cutting-edge gear, others will be decked out in cotton.

Some runners snigger at those who aren't wearing the latest, specialist clothing, but often, that cottoned-up runner is actually more sincere about running than those who look like they smeared themselves in superglue and twirled crazily around the aisles of their local running shop.

The *Code* believes that running is about running. All the other elements – kit, gadgets, etc – are secondary to the practice itself. So we should respect those who are more interested in running than in the consumerist obsession that has grown alongside it.

Don't walk in running shoes

Having said the above, the same isn't true for trainers. As sporting footwear gets increasingly more sophisticated, it becomes more important to use the right shoe for the right activity. Running shoes and walking shoes might once have been basically the same thing but that's not the case any longer. There are a number of subtle differences between the trainers you should walk in and run in. For instance, walking shoes will generally have a bit more cushioning, particularly in the heel.

What's more, before long, your running shoes will probably smell more than your normal shoes. A bit of whiff isn't a problem when you're out running but if you wear those same shoes in the office you will soon become unpopular. So, keep your forms of footwear separate: it will benefit both your walking and your running.

Wear your running bib with dignity

In the distant past, people were sensible about their race number. We would grab some safety pins and faithfully affix it to the centre of our running shirts. There it would sit throughout the race, clearly signalling that we were legitimate entrants in the event. Simple.

The running bib would also form a useful reference point for well-wishers, who could shout from the sidelines: 'Go on, 4042, you can do it!' Race photographers would also use them as a reference for when they uploaded their snaps of us looking like radiation victims fleeing an accident. It was all so straightforward.

However, more recently a terrible trend has hit the running community when it comes to race numbers. People have tried to be 'whacky' with them by pinning them on the back of their running shirt or fixing them to a running hat. Some of these 'characters' have even taken to pinning them to the front or back of their shorts. Not only is this silly, but it also risks a terrible, awkward accident. Surely there are enough dangers in this world already without putting sharp objects near your sensitive parts? I wince every time I see those safety pins so close to that region.

Full disclosure: I'm a little bit guilty of pinning my number in a silly place myself. As a member of the Vegan Runners, I would pin my running number beneath the vegan logo on my shirt because, you know, I'd hate to miss an opportunity to communicate to the world that I'm vegan.

So, just pin your running bib on sensibly and get on with the run. There's a time and a place to be whacky and during a race isn't one of them.

Don't whip your top off, men!

At what age does it become, quite literally, undesirable for men to run topless on sunny days? There is no precise science to this. Some runners maintain a trim and tasty body into middle age. Others go to pot in their early 20s.

Then there is the confusion caused by body dysmorphia: a man whose torso is worthy of a *Men's Health* cover model can easily consider himself out of shape. (I'm hoping I've got body dysmorphia.) Equally, a man who is very flabby could be kidding himself he still has a six-pack. (I've probably got that one.)

The *Code* will attempt to guide you through this minefield. It's true that there are some limited scenarios in which running without a shirt is OK. For instance, if you are taking part in one of those breast cancer charity races at which going topless is encouraged, to raise awareness. Or on the beach – but make sure you are wearing deodorant. No one wants a pongy projectile speeding past as they relax on holiday.

However, generally speaking, it's best to keep your T-shirt on, guys. The most important time this holds true is during an official running event. There have been terrible scenes of men taking off their T-shirts midway through the course and pinning the race number on to the front of their shorts. No one wants to see your nipples and no one wants you to draw attention to your ... shorts area.

So, rather than relying on an arbitrary age rule or unreliable self-perception to decide whether it's OK for you to whip off your top, why not simply ask yourself if it's *ever* a good idea to do it?

There are many reasons not to:

- You are more likely to check yourself out in any windows you pass, increasing the likelihood of a nasty collision.

- If you slip over, any graze could be that much worse.
- Yes, you could get a more even tan, but you could also get sunburned.
- If you are running through a crowded area, your slippery skin might literally touch other people's skin. They probably won't want that.
- You could make women feel uncomfortable.
- It won't even make you feel that much cooler (temperature, or otherwise).
- Speaking of which, any tattoos you may have probably aren't as cool as you hope.
- It's exercising male privilege – women aren't allowed to run topless, so why should you? (Probably very few women want to run topless, but you get the point, I hope.)

So, in summary: very few men have the sort of physique that means they can get away with running topless. If you are wondering whether you do, it's almost certain that you do not. You know, sometimes, your grandparents' clichés are actually wise: it really is better to be safe than sorry. So put your baps away, guys.

When to stop wearing skimpy vests

A related issue is when runners should stop wearing those barely-there vests – the ones that expose all of the arms. Well, as a rough rule of thumb, you should maybe stop wearing them around the same time you should stop having silly nicknames like 'Deano'.

Don't go short on your shorts

I once interviewed the Arsenal captain Tony Adams at a media event at which he had been decked out in promotional kit that included very short shorts. I suggested to Adams that we sit down for the chat and he replied: 'Let's keep standing, these shorts are ever so short and I'm worried me old potatoes might fall out.' It's an enduring image, isn't it? It often comes back to me at running events when I see male runners with barely-there shorts and worry that their old potatoes might fall out.

When the kit's got to go, it's got to go

Do you have a running shirt or pair or shorts that hold sentimental value for you and that you can't let go? Perhaps that was the garment you wore when you managed a particular milestone in your running? Or maybe it was the shirt handed to you at the end of that marathon you ran, and you want all the world to know that you have, in fact, run a marathon?

Well, one day, it will be time to move on. If the elastic goes on your shorts, you could end up showing more of yourself than is ideal. Likewise, if your T-shirt tethers you to a distant past glory then perhaps it will soon be time for you to look forward and aim for new glory.

When it comes to trainers, you need to keep replacing them because you risk injury as soon as their treads have worn out. More on that below. With regard to other running gear, the physical stakes are less high but that doesn't mean you should keep wearing the same kit every year.

Replace your running shoes regularly

Running is one of the cheaper forms of fitness. Unlike gyms, there is no monthly membership or joining fee. You don't need to buy any bats, balls or rackets and you don't need to travel anywhere to do it. You can just step outside your front door and start.

However, you do need to buy running shoes and replace them regularly. Research shows that when our running shoes become worn down, we start to change our posture and gait, which can quickly lead to injuries. This is largely due to a decline in the shoes' shock-absorption abilities.

Experts recommend you replace your running shoes every 500–750km (300–500 miles). So for instance, if you are running around 32km (20 miles) a week, you should be replacing your shoes every five months or so.

However, this mathematics is not precise because the rate at which running shoes wear down varies from person to person, and from model to model. A weightier runner who runs on rough terrain with a heavy foot strike will probably need to replace their shoes sooner than a slimmer runner who trots on smoother trails with a softer running style. Similarly, running shoes with a light, minimal style will normally wear out quicker than heavier and bulkier designs.

Therefore, rather than mechanically replacing your shoes every 650km (400 miles) or so, keep a regular look-out for telltale signs that they are causing injuries. If you start getting blisters or aches and pains, including soreness, then you might be due a new pair. Or you can check the grooves and treads on the base of the shoes, like you might with a car tyre. If they're seriously worn down then get rid of them.

Another way is to check the midsole. If you press your thumb into the midsole it should feel soft and spongy. If it feels tough, that might mean the cushioning has compressed and the shoe is no longer giving you the support you need.

Once you know that your trainers have seen better days, invest in a new pair as soon as you can. We don't need to spend much money on running but safe running shoes are kind of non-negotiable.

PS – don't take any of the above as an excuse to keep splashing the cash in running shops just because a new model has come on to the market. You should have a loving relationship with your running shoes, so never ditch your existing pair before their time. Don't be like one of those old billionaire love-rats, forever dumping their girlfriends for a younger model.

It's OK to sniff new running shoes

In fact, it's more or less compulsory. So as you take them out of the box, pop your nose inside the shoes and inhale with glee.

Why do people do this? Experts say this is because the smell of new trainers is a positive scent associated with luxury and indulgence. We have bought new shoes so we are already in a happy state. So although it might seem weird, you can inhale and enjoy, knowing it's a perfectly natural thing. Sniff, sniff and sniff again!

Check your tights in the mirror

Running tights are tricky things. Some people can absolutely rock them, others should never go anywhere near them.

Manufacturers say they can stabilise your muscles, keep your legs dry and compress to give your legs extra support. Some of the most serious runners at any event wear them, so they must be good, right?

Well, up to a point. The harsh reality is that some people look great and appropriate in running tights, but others look awful and even, ahem, highly inappropriate in running tights. Men in particular should consider whether they have the right ... physiology to wear such ... revealing garments.

One way of approaching this is to pose in them in front of a mirror before you leave your home. If you don't like what you see, just pop a pair of shorts over the top and the problem will be solved.

HOW TO BE A CONSIDERATE RUNNER

Running is generally not a team game so it is easy to become a bit self-centred about it all. The solitude of running is one of its joys for many of us but the *Code* knows you don't want to be that selfish runner whom everyone secretly hates. You only have to look at how many people have begun to feel about cyclists to see how quickly an athletic community can become disliked.

So here is your *Code* for how to run considerately. Find out how to avoid run rage, how to post about your runs on social media without boring people to tears and why it's time for men to stop staring at women in running kit.

You can also find out why you shouldn't snot or spit during a run. I would have hoped that no one would need to be told this but the evidence of the world suggests otherwise. By the time you've read this section, you'll hopefully know all about the right etiquette.

THE RUNNER AT HOME

Shocking as this fact is, our non-running relatives are not as interested in our running as we are. Naturally, we will feel that this is mere envy on their part: they just can't cope with the fact that they have such an athletic hero in their midst, so they feign disinterest to get one over on us.

Well, it might be that, or it might just be that we're simply not as interesting as we thought. Whatever the reason, though, runners can certainly be annoying to our non-running family members. Here is how to coexist with them in harmony.

Clear away your smelly kit

After a long, exhausting run it feels great to peel off your kit, chuck it on the floor and sink into a nice relaxing bath, but the people you share your home with don't want sweaty, smelly garments lying around. So put your used gear in the laundry basket or straight into the wash, and keep your trainers tucked away somewhere.

Make time for the family

Studies show that popular times for running include early in the morning on weekdays and throughout the morning on Saturdays. It's probably just a coincidence that these are the times parents are getting the kids ready for school, or driving them to and from their weekend club activities... If you want to remain popular, don't use running as way of dodging responsibility.

Lie in from time to time

Speaking of responsibility, it's unlikely you'll be performing your ... marital duties if every time your partner wakes up, you're already out there, pounding the early morning streets. You're also probably disturbing them much earlier than they'd like every time your alarm goes off at the crack of dawn.

Don't talk about running all the time

Your family doesn't care about your split times, the elevation levels on your new route or the fact that you've 'got a long run in the morning'. If you need to talk about running, sign up for a running club or join a Facebook group. It can be great to talk about your passion but save it for people who care!

Don't bore people

Coming in from a run is one of the best feelings in the world. You have achieved the goal you set out to reach, your body and mind feel alive and buzzing. Everything feels right. Running can clear the mind and remove mental obstacles. Fresh insights can pop into your head, which you might never have managed had you not gone out and pounded the pavements for an hour or two.

In these moments, we can feel almost evangelical. We want the world to see life how we do. We can find it hard to imagine that anyone could be anything less than fascinated by the run we've just nailed. Our energy is such that we are exhilarated and able to hold court dramatically and at some length.

But just wait a moment. While you've been out running, the people you live with haven't been sitting anxiously by the window, awaiting your triumphant return. They've been getting on with their own lives (I know, I know – the cheek of them!) and probably doing all sorts of boring tasks that you've dodged by going out.

Even cheekier yet, they are also not wanting to hear about the minutiae of your running. Nor, in all likelihood, are they going to want to hear about the paradigm-shifting insight that struck you in mile eight. (Because, much like the dream you had last night, it won't be as amazing as you think it is.)

So don't chew their ears off. A good way of returning gently from a run is to walk for five minutes after you've finished, rather than bursting through the door moments after your final step.

Don't bully your family into joining you

There is a fine line between being enthusiastic and being pushy. Don't try to drag your partner, kids or other housemates out with you. If they want to run, they'll tell you.

Don't be generally repulsive

Got chafing on your inner thighs? These things happen, but don't apply cream to your nether regions as others are having their breakfast.

Dispose of toenail clippings

Toenails seem like trifling little things but they can cause a lot of problems for runners. From subungual hematoma (blackish-red and bruised nails to you or me), to onychauxis (when they go yellow), onychocryptosis (when the nail cuts into the skin) and onychomycosis (crumbly nails), they really can be a pain in the ... well, in the foot.

A lot of problems can be avoided by keeping your feet clean and the nails trimmed. The best time to trim nails is during a bath or shower, or shortly after, when they are softened by the heat. However, this has a tendency to lead to people leaving their clippings hanging about in the bathroom.

We all know deep down that our dreams may be fascinating to us but they are boring to everyone else. It's the same with your toenail clippings – they might seem fine to you but to other people they are monumentally ewww. So, do everyone a favour and dispose of them promptly. Please and thank you.

Running and social media guidelines

WE'RE TAUGHT AS children that it's nice to share but when it comes to social media, that's not always true. More than 66 million posts are tagged #running on Instagram and the world could have survived without a lot of them. That said, according to a survey for the website RunnersRadar, runners who post their runs on social media are more likely to run 5km (3 miles) faster than those who do not, so perhaps there is a good reason for doing it.

Knowing what to post and what not to post is a skill. The problem for runners is that we are never less in tune with that skill than just after we've finished a run, when we're full of pride and enthusiasm.

While the average pace you just achieved on your 5km (3-mile) morning run might be fascinating to you, for your online friends it can be indescribably boring. Some non-running tweeters have even muted the words 'run' and 'running' because they're so fed up of hearing from us.

But even if your running posts do get a few 'likes,' don't let that go to your head. Too many runners have started to tailor their entire running for social media validation. They end up running more regularly than they should, or running faster than they should, all in pursuit of online 'likes'. Before long, the only updates they are posting are from the physiotherapy clinic.

So how do you avoid become a tiresome tweeter? Here are some rules and boundaries.

Posts that are OK

- When something exceptional has happened, such as your fastest ever pace or longest ever distance.
- When you passed a significant milestone, such as your 800th kilometre (500th mile) this year.
- Any post on Strava – that's what it's there for.
- Posts about bad runs. These are part of the running experience and it's refreshing to tell the world that not every run is a perfect experience. So if you've had a bad time, don't be scared to share it.
- A photo of your run in a genuinely stunning or interesting location.
- Encouraging, self-aware comments left under the posts of newcomers to running.
- Any post that passes this filter: imagine you are sitting in the pub with your friends, and only post something on social media that you would say to them.

- Puffed-up posts – 'While you lot have been lazing in bed some of us have been out here running a half marathon!'
- Bragging posts – no one likes a show-off, so please don't post endlessly about your achievements in that aggressive, preening way that some people (well, some men) do.
- Serial posts – the day before an 18-miler you post that you are going to run an 18-miler tomorrow. During the 18-miler you post that you are running an 18-miler. After the 18-miler, you post that you just ran an 18-miler. Come on, this isn't *Coronation Street*.
- Dangerous posts – never try to take a selfie as you are actually running – it's dangerous for you and others.
- Excessively hashtagged posts – it's fine to use a few hashtags but only a few. Once you're into double figures you're probably overdoing it and if '#blessed' is one of them, you definitely are.

THE RUNNER OUT AND ABOUT

When you are pounding the pavements you are an ambassador for the running community. Non-runners will judge us all on how you interact with them. So be nice to them and be nice to your fellow runners. Here's how.

Don't spit or snot

There's no polite way of putting it: some people like to spit and fire out snot bombs when they run. Footballers are infamous for this practice but runners can be just as guilty of it.

It's never been a good time to behave that way but in the Covid era and afterwards it's particularly important not to. This habit is 'very dangerous' according to Bert Blocken, professor at Eindhoven University in the Netherlands and KU Leuven in Belgium. He says the danger is particularly acute when it involves mucus, which can contain a 'high dose' of viruses. 'If someone is running or walking close behind you and you spit out saliva or mucus then you are putting them at risk,' says the prof.

And look, it's also just a really unpleasant habit, so maybe runners could cut it out completely? If you really need to spit, move to the side of the path or street and make sure you're at least 1.8m (6ft) (but preferably more) away from others. To avoid the issue arising in the first place, carry tissues for spit and mucus and dispose of them promptly and safely after your run.

Conversational etiquette

Chatting while you're running can be a great way to take your mind off the strain you're putting your body through. But remember, if you are running alongside a less fit runner, it's unkind to ask them questions if they are out of breath and you're not. A bit of empathy goes a long way.

Don't be a jangler

If you're taking your keys and loose change out on a run with you then try to stop them jangling. It can be annoying for other runners to have that sound following them round the course. Pack them tightly. You can also watch for other unintended noise: synthetic kit and jewellery are two common offenders.

Don't use park benches to tie up laces

Would you wipe the underside of your running shoes on your duvet? I hope the answer is a definite 'no'. I mean, who knows what traces of dog poo and other hell you've trodden on? I also hope that you therefore don't stick your foot up on to a park bench to tie up your laces. Remember, someone will want to sit there.

Avoid run rage

Everyone knows cyclists can be a grumpy bunch. Social media is full of tales and videos of angry, Lycra-clad cyclists shrieking at motorists and slamming their fists on the bonnets of their cars.

It is also widely accepted that drivers can also be angry. Road rage incidents range from gratuitous use of the horn to loud swearing and actual murder.

But runners can be just as testy. I've seen joggers out on solo runs scream at pedestrians to 'get out of the way', thump cars after their drivers somehow upset them, and even, in one memorable case, swear furiously at a passing duck.

One year at the Windsor Half Marathon, a runner aggressively elbowed me out of the way in the first mile. Before he ran off, he locked me with psychotic eyes and shouted that if I couldn't go faster I should get out of the way. My 8-minute mile pace was more than respectable, but even had I been plodding along slowly, this behaviour was completely out of proportion.

I've also seen flashpoints at so called 'fun' parkrun events. These are designed to be community affairs, where everyone from pupils to pensioners and pelters to plodders are welcomed. Unfortunately, 'rage runners' can also be found at them. At Fulham Palace parkrun, a red-faced man, who was running with his terrified child strapped into a pram, deliberately slammed the pram into me as we turned a corner, before snarling and speeding off, shouting angrily at other runners as he went. Poor kid.

Race organisers also report countless episodes of angry runners shouting at them about small issues, such as their finishers' T-shirt not being the right size. It's not OK.

Runners could reduce the risk of confrontation by choosing their routes more thoughtfully. For a gentle 5km (3-mile) jog, busy public areas might be suitable, but for a draining 20km (12.5-mile) run, it might be best to opt for a more secluded course, particularly for the latter stages, to avoid the culture clash of running pumped yet exhausted down a busy shopping street.

Another step could be for us runners everywhere to just get over ourselves. The narcissism that prompts many joggers to share hellishly boring details of their every run on social networks is similar to the one that makes some feel that the pavement belongs to them. We need to calm down and remind ourselves that it is not the responsibility of pedestrians to accommodate our heroic pursuit.

If you can't run without getting angry, you should pause your running until you have sorted out your head.

What if ...
someone shouts abuse from a car?

If you run regularly, this will probably have happened to you. You're running along, loving life, and someone shouts at you from a passing car. There are various ways to respond. One is to make a gesture back, either with your face, your voice or your hand. In the moment, this often feels like the most instinctive way to go.

Some runners suggest calling out the chorus of an annoying, catchy song, so it gets stuck in the head of the shouter all day. Possible contenders for this include 'Who Let The Dogs Out', or any annoying advertising jingle.

It's important to put safety first, though. The sort of person who shouts something unpleasant from a car is probably not the happiest or nicest person in the world. Beware: there have been reports of these situations escalating when a runner reacted to one of the bores.

Also, sometimes you might have misheard what is shouted. One runner I know thought a stranger was hurling abuse at him, so he gave it back to them with both barrels. Only when they arrived home did he realise it had been his neighbours, shouting encouragement. That runner was me. So if you possibly can, just ignore any shouting and let hecklers pass.

If you want to lessen the chances of someone shouting at you, anecdotal evidence suggests that wearing headphones lessens the chances of you being targeted this way. So, even if you don't plan to listen to anything, plugging them in for your run might mean the shouters leave you alone.

Be nice to newbie runners

You were the new one, once. Be nice to the newbies. For some people, their first tentative runs are vulnerable experiences. They worry that they are doing it wrong, or that they look stupid, or that they might slip over. They feel like they will be laughed at as slowcoaches. The more runners there are, the better the world will be. Make sure you give them a bit of love, so they stick around.

Stop staring at women in running kit

Over the years, running kit for both genders has become sleeker and more minimalist. This has helped runners of all genders to keep cool on hot days and made us more aerodynamic. All of this is generally good news.

What is less good news is the effect it has had on women runners. As the runners line up at parkrun and other communal running events, some men's gazes stray towards the armless T-shirts and tight running shorts that women are wearing.

Various response tips have been given to women. Some say that if a man is staring at them then the best thing to do is to stare right back at him. Others suggest that the woman simply calls out what the man is doing. But also, how about men took a lead on this? How about simply not staring at women and making them uncomfortable?

Women have been through a lot to get treated with respect in the world of running. The incredible truth is that women were once banned from taking part in long-distance running events, since it was considered that they were too weak or fragile. It wasn't until the 1960s that this began to change. In 1961, a 19-year-old runner, Julia Chase, entered a 10.5km (6.5-

mile) road race in Chicopee, Massachusetts, in an attempt to challenge the ban. Even then, her efforts were trivialised by one media write-up of the time, which said: 'Eyewitnesses report her other dimensions are very good.'

A few years later, in 1967, Kathrine Switzer, a student, became the first woman to officially run the Boston Marathon. Amazingly, the race organiser chased after her and tried to push her off the course.

In the 1970s, the Amateur Athletic Union allowed women to register for marathons, but they were ordered to start at a separate time or starting line than men. In the 1972 New York City Marathon, women refused to obey and sat down for 10 minutes at the starting line in protest.

During the 1990s, however, *Runner's World* magazine reported that for the first time the majority of its new subscribers were women. Women also began to make up the majority of participants at large running events. For instance, the 1998 Rock 'n' Roll Marathon in San Diego reported that 55 per cent of the entries were women.

So it's been quite a journey so far for women and running. Maybe men could stop being creepy towards them.

How often to ask for sponsorship

WE'VE ALL SEEN it happen. Someone proudly announces on social media that they are planning to take on a running challenge to raise funds for their favourite charity. 'Oh look,' we think, bursting with admiration, 'Peter's doing a half marathon for an orphans' charity. How lovely of him!'

▷

A few days later, Peter posts his fundraising page again. 'Ah yes, Peter's running for the orphans,' we recall. 'Hope it goes well for him. Must remember to drop him a tenner when I've got my credit card handy.'

When he posts again the following morning, you start to feel a little nagged but you remind yourself that it's for a good cause. It's all good.

But in the weeks that follow, as Peter repeatedly posts his fundraising page on social media, our tolerance is worn down until we find ourselves wanting to scream: 'Oh, shut up, just shut up! And sod the sodding orphans too!'

(There is a sequel to this epic of annoyance when Peter returns four months later with the 'exciting news' that he has just entered the Paris marathon. And you'll never guess what...)

Just as one man's terrorist is another man's freedom fighter, so is one man's selfless charity hero another man's vain boaster. There is a fine line between being a plucky raiser of funds and awareness for a good cause and being a bore who destroys people's sympathy by holding out the virtual begging bowl a few too many times.

Here are the times when it is definitely acceptable to post your fundraising page:

1 When you first set up the page you can announce your plan and ask friends and followers to sponsor you.

2 A week or two later, perhaps following a particularly significant training run, you can follow up.

3 The morning of the event itself is a good time to do a post that includes your link.

4 Afterwards, why not post a picture of your medal, with a reminder of why you did the run?

All of those times are entirely acceptable. Other times will be, too, but each time you are posting outside of those four examples, you are risking becoming a fundraising bore, so you need to tread carefully.

The JustGiving website advises users that posting their fundraising page 'three times a week is acceptable' but friends and followers of fundraisers nearly always think otherwise.

The trick with fundraising can be to focus on quality rather than quantity. If you make each of your online posts interesting, original and creative, few people will object to seeing them and they'll be more likely to cough up.

In other words, five thoughtful and interesting posts are better than 50 repetitive 'Yeah, so just another reminder I'm doing this charity run and I'd love you to sponsor me' posts.

Be aware of sharp corners

These are hotspots for accidental collisions because people on both sides cannot see the other one coming. So approach carefully and be alert! See below...

Stay alert

One of the joys of running is that it can take you into a hypnotic state. A study found that more than half of runners experience a trance-like experience as they pound the pavements. Running can, then, be blissful but it's still very important to stay alert as you trot. If you accidentally bump into a pedestrian, you put both of you at the risk of infection and the health service can't afford to treat unnecessary injuries from runners who switched off and tripped over an obstacle.

Be nice to pedestrians – particularly during a pandemic

Sticking with pedestrians – running feels such a virtuous activity that it's easy for us to forget that not everyone is as keen on our special hobby. Some people have always found us annoying and the Covid-19 pandemic ripped the lid off that resentment.

Government restrictions during the first lockdown seemed to heighten tensions between runners and the rest of society. Never mind Leavers and Remainers, a new culture war was fought between joggers and walkers. As Britain went into lockdown in spring 2020, the London editor of *The Irish Times* described 'public outrage' in the capital over runners 'who have been panting along ... refusing to get out of the way for pedestrians in case they lose half a second off their time'.

At the heart of tensions between joggers and pedestrians was a simple question: should the onus be on us or them to make space? But what we all want in the end is a world where everyone is considerate. So don't get caught up in the power games – just take the lead and be the nice one.

To avoid alarm and the risk of infection, when you pass someone, give them as wide a berth as you safely can, and don't return on to the path until you are at least 10m (33ft) ahead.

A thing I love about running: Most of all, I love how running makes me feel. A run can be so therapeutic. I love the challenge of running. During the coronavirus lockdown I ran 300km (185 miles) in a single month to raise funds for Headway, which works to improve life after brain injury. Those runs will live long in my memory but every run is special in its own way. Pretty much every time I return after a run I feel better in my body and mind for having done it.

A thing I hate about running: I am less keen on how much motivation it takes to get out there. Even though I know full well that a run will make me feel better, some days it still takes a lot of motivation for me to get off the sofa, put my running shoes on and do some miles. During my years as a professional footballer, there was no decision to make: we trained or played every day and I had to be there. Now I'm retired, I have to motivate myself. That's easier said than done, particularly during Scottish winters when it's dark and rainy. I sometimes wish there was a magic wand that would make me motivated to run every day. I know I'd feel better for it.

Simon is a former Celtic, Sheffield Wednesday, St Johnstone, Dunfermline, Partick Thistle and Scotland football international.

Don't text or make calls while you're running

Running used to be an absolute sanctuary of an experience in the time before mobile phones existed. The moment you shut your front door behind you and took your first step, you left all the hassles of life behind. As you ran along, nobody could contact you and you could not contact anyone. It was your blissful headspace but also a blissful physical space. The world and its hassles just couldn't touch you while you were out there. You were free.

Even when the first mobile phones were invented, most runners left them at home when they went out. Although having a phone on you could be a sensible safety precaution, a lot of us were actually still happy to remain uncontactable.

However, the advent of smartphones has changed a lot. It makes a lot of sense for us to take out phones on the run. They contain our music, our podcasts, our running apps and our cameras. In some ways, this is a good thing but it also opens the way for some dangerous behaviour because there is no worse time to send a text to someone than in the middle of a run. Many a friendship has been sullied or work drama deepened by someone sending an ill-advised message while pounding the pavements.

You are pumped up, you've just spent time alone, plodding along while you mull over an issue and in that moment you might not be at your most diplomatic. With your adrenalin raised and your heart pumping, you won't be in the best state to send out a judicious message.

Runners have been known to have ticked off their bosses, sent a way too confident invitation to a date to someone they fancied or started an online war with their neighbour, all because they sent out a text message midway through a run. Had they waited until they got home and chilled out a bit, they would either have engaged differently, or not engaged at all.

In the same vein, sometimes when your schedule is busy, you can be tempted to multitask by catching up on phone calls while you're out there pounding the pavement. Now, from your point of view, this can seem a good idea. It kills two birds with one stone and it's easy to imagine that you look important and powerful as you stride along, barking away into your AirPods. Also, the conversation can distract you from the effort of running. That makes *three* birds with one stone.

So yes, making phone calls during a run seems a brilliant idea for the runner but to the person at the other end of the line it is a far less attractive prospect. The chances are you will be breathless and pumped up, and few people want phone calls from a breathless or pumped-up person. Or if they do, they probably had a different kind of conversation in mind.

There's also an arrogance to it. By calling on the trot, you are sending out the message that you needed to squeeze this phone call into your schedule, whereas the person you are calling doesn't need to. It's a really wanky power move, and unless you are looking to make a really wanky power move, it's best avoided.

So unless it's an emergency, or unless you have the sincere, prior approval of the person at the other end of the line, keep running and phoning separate.

Pee considerately

LET'S GET THE simple truths out of the way first: when you have to go, you have to go. There are no two ways about it. During long training runs and at big running events, this can be an awkward problem. The question is: how can we answer the call of nature with dignity and decency?

We've all seen the scores of men, lined up against bushes or walls, taking a pee midway through a running

▶

event. I'll hazard a guess that few, if any, of the female runners who have spent months preparing for that event and possibly travelled many miles to get there did so in the hope that they could spot skinny men and their trails of waste fluid.

I've seen some astonishing sights. I once saw a man move just a few yards off the trail of a parkrun course and simply pee into mid-air, with no attempt to be discreet. We all just had to look the other way. It was only a 5km (3-mile) run, how desperate could he have been? Then there was the woman who was running ahead of me at the Dublin Marathon, who suddenly stopped dead in the middle of the road, shouted: 'Ah, f**k it' and squatted down on the floor for an actual poo. At a half marathon, I saw a woman squat down for a quick pee. When the flow was finished, she realised her leg muscles and joints had seized up and she couldn't get up. She had to wait there, hovering over her puddle, until some stewards could help her away, like an injured frog.

Those sorts of scenes are far from ideal but we shouldn't judge the protagonists, particularly the female ones, because there is a disparity here. Whereas men can simply hop off the course and answer the call of nature against a tree or in some bushes, it's not so easy or acceptable for women. They are forced to wait until they reach the next batch of portaloos and then queue for those facilities, which can be chambers of hell at the best of times.

So, what to do when you have to go? Here are some etiquette guidelines:

- Hold it in if you can comfortably manage that. Some studies say people can hold pee for two to three hours.

▷

- Don't drink too much. Sure, you must be adequately hydrated for running and on a long run you will want regular top-ups, but don't drink drastically high levels of fluid. The average adult bladder has a volume of around 300–400ml (10–13.5fl oz).
- But also, don't drink too little. This seems counterintuitive in this context but drinking too little can make you pee more. Dehydration concentrates your urine, irritating the sensitive lining of your bladder, and giving you the urge to go.
- Caffeine is a diuretic, so take it easy with your pre-run espressos and fizzy energy drinks. Sure, they'll give you a boost but they might also mean you offset any speed advantage with regular pit stops.
- Some sugary snacks and energy gels can also send you that way, particularly the first few times you have them. This is because they can cause mini contractions as your bladder tries to get rid of all that unfamiliar sweetness.
- If you are queuing for toilets during a running event, make sure the queue doesn't snake into the path of the runners. Let them flow as you wait to flow.
- Sometimes, runners prefer to not stop as they pee. As inexplicable as this seems to non-runners (and to many runners, too) they will simply let go as they stride along. Even if you are not embarrassed by doing this, for the sake of others, try to conceal what you've done. You can throw water over yourself, so you look generally wet, rather than having a telltale patch of shame. (When it rains, Mother Nature will take care of this for you.) And if this is something you'd consider doing, make sure you bring a change of clothes...

GUEST FEATURE *Martin Yelling*

A thing I love about running: I love the way that running works with you through all the seasons of your life, if you let it. It shapes and supports you, it drives, challenges and encourages you, it rewards and cares for you. It can make you feel better, be fitter and healthier physically and mentally, and it can be your best friend and your worst enemy! The journey of learning to harness the opportunity of running for a lifetime is a challenge worth embracing!

A thing I hate about running: Portaloos at mile 24 of a marathon. I mean, no one should spend too long in one of these. It's simply not safe or sensible! The trouble is, once you sit down with marathon legs it's so terribly tricky to get up again in a hurry.

Martin Yelling is a former international runner, elite duathlete and triathlete. He is the co-author of Running in the Midpack: How to be a Strong, Successful and Happy Runner.

Don't swear at running events

Running can be painful and frustrating at times. You might pull a muscle, or suddenly get cramp. It hurts! Equally, you might see a mile marker during a long running event and be disappointed you haven't run further. Or you might look down at your running watch and realise you're not managing the sort of pace you'd trained so hard to achieve.

In any of these scenarios, the temptation may be to curse. There are few better ways of dealing with pain or disappointment than a good swear, right? But not so fast: what if there are kids running in the event, too? Or what if there are families standing by the side of the event, cheering on the runners?

So watch your language when you're running around other people. A sly swear under the breath is fine but nothing louder than that. It's probably best to follow this basic rule: never shout anything that you wouldn't say in front of your grandmother.

Don't breathe creepily

Breathing is as important in running as it is in life. So never apologise for breathing during your runs. However, what is less forgivable is the heavy breather. Nearly always a middle-aged man, this runner will pant and deep-breathe his way around the course, sounding like an approaching pervert to those behind him.

It's easy to joke but it can be scary for other runners and even scarier for people who are just out for an afternoon stroll and suddenly hear a panting man approaching them from behind. It is good manners to pay attention to your breathing.

Don't be condescending to older runners

Anyone who has lined up at a running event has seen the runner whose fitness and form belies their advanced years. You know the type: the greying pensioner who somehow manages to outpace people less than half their age.

There are plenty of them around: at the 2017 Boston Marathon, 221 of the 27,488 starters were over the age of 70. It can feel tempting to smile condescendingly at the older runners as you all line up at the start of a run. What a triumph for the human spirit, you think, that such a decaying old bag would dare show up to a running event! Best give them a smile because the old dear probably won't know what's hit them once it all starts!

Try to resist that temptation, though, because once it all starts you realise that they are better runners than you. It should be them giving you a pitying smile, if anything! And listen, even if they are slowcoaches, the last thing they need is a commiserating look from a youngster. They've seen and experienced more in their life than you, so don't be condescending.

Don't patronise younger runners

In the same vein as above, you might think you look like a wise guru as you pat a kid on the head, telling them 'well done' for managing to complete the 5K event in your local park, but to them you might well appear as a sad oldie, confused by the passage of time. Also, the chances are that in no time at all they will have found their feet and will be whizzing past you as you huff along.

Go easy with the unsolicited advice

Every gathering of runners seems to have an unsolicited coach in its number. The man (it's always a man) who wanders around other runners, giving them tips to improve their running. He believes he is just being kind as he offers the benefit of his years of running.

For some of those on the receiving end of that advice it will have been an act of kindness, but for others, the advice will be less welcome. Perhaps they are quite happy with their 27-minute finish time for a 5K and aren't chomping at the bit to aim for a sub-20-minute finish. The unsolicited coach won't consider this.

There is a fine line between selflessly offering genuine advice and egotistically showing people how much better than them you are. The unsolicited coach frequently dances on to the wrong side of this divide.

Sometimes, people will ignore their advice and the unsolicited coach will be upset. Other times, the runners will benefit from it, and the unsolicited coach won't be able to resist reminding them of their role. He'll be waiting at the finishing line to say: 'See! What did I tell you? What did I tell you?'

Greet other runners

We've all been there. You're running along having a lovely time and then you see a fellow runner heading towards you. The question immediately thumps its way into your head: should I greet them or not?

The dilemma is understandable. Part of you wants to wave, smile or say 'hi'. Maybe all three at once? It's lovely to be friendly to anyone and fellow runners, even when they are not known to us, are kind of like family. It makes the world a better place when strangers greet one another. So why the hell not give them a friendly wave?

Simultaneously, other thoughts are coming into your head. Will it look creepy, or needy, if I greet them? Maybe they don't want a stranger waving at them. What if, horror of horrors, you wave and they don't acknowledge you? You'll be stung by the social shame of being blanked and will need to immediately change your running route so you never, ever see the runner again.

As you continue to get closer to that awkward moment when you pass one another your entire identity is put on the line, when you find out whether you are a nice person (by waving) and whether you are a cool person (whether they acknowledge you or not). It can turn into quite a tense inner monologue as you approach.

Often, all that (over)thinking is the biggest problem. So why not simplify it by deciding, once and for all, whether you are a waver or not. Once you've done that, stick with that decision every time. Either wave every time, or never wave.

Only you can decide whether you want to be a greeter or a non-greeter. Personally, I am a greeter. That said, there are times when you need to be mindful of the other runner. What feels like a friendly greeting to you might feel threatening to a lone female jogger – particularly if you are closing in on their personal space. Sometimes a quick nod is better than a full on greeting.

In this ever-more divided world, we need more connection, not less. But a bit of empathy for runners who might feel threatened or creeped out by a greeting from an overly-friendly stranger goes a long way, too.

Don't shout 'coming through'

Seriously, just don't. If you can't make your way safely around a pedestrian or slower runner at your current pace, just slow down. It won't be the end of the world.

Shut up about your running club

Double-glazing salesmen can be a pushy bunch. In their desperation to sign you up to their movement, they will press you hard. They're not the only proselytisers, though. Every running club seems to have one member who considers it their life's work to encourage every runner they meet to join up.

They start by talking to people at parkrun. Wearing their running club's T-shirt, they approach strangers and ask them why they're not a member yet. Then they stand at the finishing line of a bigger event, with leaflets and a manic smile, chanting the name of the local running club like some sort of Vedic mantra.

Before long, they lose the plot completely and start approaching runners in the park. They're *this* close to a restraining order.

Tolerate stupid well-wishers

The well-wishers and supporters who stand at the side of the road during running events can be absolutely lovely. But they can also be absolutely stupid. When you are 5km (3 miles) into a marathon, it can grate when a well-wisher shouts out: 'Well done, you're nearly there!' You are absolutely not 'nearly there'. What the hell are they playing at?

Similarly, one can feel a little patronised when someone stands at the sidelines of a short run and treats the event like an Ironman Triathlon. Perhaps you have encountered the sort I mean: the well-meaning mother who stands at the side of a parkrun and tells runners who are covering a mere 5km (3 miles) that 'you're all heroes!'

What must it be like living with such people? As you successfully make a cup of tea, do they whack the *Chariots of Fire* soundtrack on and run in slow motion towards you, with a bravery trophy to present to you for your remarkable achievement? As you mow the lawn, do they stand on the patio whooping encouragement and praise, as tears of pride gush down their face? 'Well done! Go you!'

Then there is the other sod of the sidelines: the 'keep going' person. It's such banal advice, especially when it is offered early on in a race. If you've spent months, or possibly longer, preparing for a half marathon, it's very unlikely that in mile two you will forget to keep going.

A close relative of this is the man who shouts 'Go on!' over and over at runners who are, quite literally, already 'going on'. We've got 'going on' covered already. You might as well tell us to 'get out of bed' or 'breathe' because we've already got those tasks under control, too.

But the point is that we should tolerate all these well-wishers because well is all they are wishing us. There is enough darkness and division in this world without us turning against people who give up hours of their time to support runners, or at least to try to support us, however silly some of them might be. Imagine big running events without smiling faces on the sidelines – they would be a much less warming experience, right? So let's cherish them all.

PS – The greatest well-wisher I have ever personally encountered at a running event was at the Dublin Marathon. It was an old man standing at the side, calling out over and over: 'Just tink about the Guinness ... just tink about the Guinness ... just tink about the Guinness...' At the finish, I noticed quite a few runners hobbling into a nearby pub. They must have been tinking about the Guinness.

A thing I love about running: I love the little life-affirming moments that can appear in the depths of struggle and despair. I was in a 24-hour race on a 1-mile loop and had been vomiting from early on. Somewhere around 4 a.m. I shuffled half-blind with fatigue and dehydration towards a hardy supporter standing at the side of the course. 'You're looking good!' she said enthusiastically, her voice loud in the night.

At the pace I was moving I had plenty of time to consider this. 'Really?' I asked, incredulous. She took a few moments to think about it. 'Well, compared to later,' she said with a smile. It was impossible not to laugh. And it helped, at least for a little while.

A thing I hate about running: There are those special days when running feels suddenly effortless. We watch, stunned, as the earth flashes by. Our legs are miraculously fresh, our joints are refurbed and even our glutes do whatever glutes are supposed to do beyond filling our shorts. It is a surprising and wonderful thing.

But every sunbeam has its shadow and every dream run has its evil twin: the day when gravity increases and the surface of the earth has turned to toffee. Headwinds are perpetual, the air is thick and the GPS satellites send lies to our watch. On these days, legs are disinterested, joints are prematurely aged and we realise that whatever a glute does, it is clearly not doing it today.

On these less wondrous days we can only persevere and do our best. We might even think, that's it, enough, but once we are home the memory fades and we begin to dream of better runs to come. Because if we runners are anything, we are optimists.

Michael is an athlete, writer and speaker who ran 250km (155 miles) in 24 hours around an athletics track. @michaelstocksrunner

RUN WITH YOUR CONSCIENCE

Running is a largely solitary pursuit but that doesn't mean it has to be a selfish one. There are many ways to do good as you run.

Be the change you want to see

Gandhi wore robes, you wear polyester. But you should follow his famous quote when you're out on a run, and try to 'be the change you want to see in the world'. So rather than asking 'Why should I always be the one who gives way?', relish the fact that you are being that person.

Plogging

Running in nature is a wonderful experience – until you notice all the litter that is strewn across our parks, riverbanks and streets. Well, plogging is the answer! This eco-friendly fitness trend, which started in Scandinavia, combines jogging with picking up rubbish (*plocka upp* means 'pick up' in Swedish).

Fundraising

Thanks to the astonishing growth of JustGiving and other fundraising platforms, sponsored runs are now a part of the online scene. More than £4 billion has been raised on JustGiving since it was launched in 2000.

Fundraising pages remain a win-win option. Charities get much-needed funds and awareness, and the runner gets motivation to take their training seriously. (But as already mentioned, do try to avoid being one of those people who share their page on Facebook every blooming day!)

GoodGym

Loneliness is a serious problem for many elderly people but this group has found a solution that pairs runners with pensioners. Volunteers run to the homes of older people to help with one-off practical tasks, or simply to keep them company. It's a virtuous circle: you get increased motivation to run, the elderly person gets company and help.

GUEST FEATURE *Anji Andrews*

A thing I love about running: It's so hard to choose just one thing. Running is where I find my peace, settle arguments with myself, prove to myself that I can do anything on days where there is doubt. As someone who usually runs solo, running gives me community, especially in my role with GoodGym Newcastle where we combine physical activity with volunteering. Running connects me to people I would never have known, in places I would have never been. It's one of the few true pathways in life where you get out of it what you put in. The purity of running in an often overstimulated world is what keeps me going back for more.

A thing I hate about running: Even the heartbreak of missing out on events through injury or coming up short on race day can't dampen the enjoyment of running for me. I don't know if this is because I have had long-term spells of injury and illness in my 11 years of running but even on days where I feel like I am running through porridge, and the weather is awful, I can still find something to find happiness in. Whether that's the joy of the hot shower afterwards, or the fact I faced a private battle to just keep going when I wanted to stop, there is always something. I have thought long and hard about this and apart from cleaning my trainers almost every day during the winter, there is nothing I dislike about running.

Anji Andrews is the co-author of **Running in the Midpack: How to be a Strong, Successful and Happy Runner.**

Become a 'guide runner'

Only 10.4 per cent of adults with a visual impairment take part in sport once a week, compared to 36.1 per cent of non-disabled adults. Guide runners are the volunteers who help the visually impaired to join in our favourite hobby. The role became famous during the London 2012 Paralympics but it is now something any runner can do because England Athletics and British Blind Sport have launched a national database that connects visually impaired adults with guide runners.

Keep it local

Parkrun tourism and travelling for marathons in faraway destinations can be fun but all that driving and flying takes its toll on the environment. So next time you're choosing a marathon, consider a local option. Also, why not jog, rather than drive, to parkrun each Saturday morning – you'll get a great warm-up.

Get the right gear

The morally bankrupt supply chains of some major sportswear manufacturers have nagged away at the conscience of many a runner. Did a kid in a sweatshop make my running vest?

Then there is the environmental impact: a 2013 study by the Massachusetts Institute of Technology found a pair of running shoes was responsible for 13.6kg (30lb) of carbon emissions because each shoe is made up of 65 separate parts requiring more than 360 steps to assemble.

Don't despair, there are ethically sound options. Manufacturers such as BAM and Patagonia offer environmentally friendly kit options. Patagonia also makes regular checks on labour conditions in its factories. Sundried make their kit from used coffee grounds and plastic bottles. Howies, a small company in Wales, use 100 per cent renewable electricity and have a high-standards certification on labour rights in factories.

Even better, the big players are finally catching up, too: Adidas have released trainers with a Parley upper, made from recycled plastic from the sea. So do a bit of research – it does wonders for the conscience, and the world.

Paul Hobrough

A thing I love about running:

People. People who run are simply nicer human beings than those who don't. Not because they are fitter, or look better or may well live longer. They are nicer just because they have purpose, have perspective and are happier about life. This does come with a caveat however ... some of the rudest and most depressed people I have ever met are runners who are unable to run due to injury/illness at that moment in time. Those who say 'there is nothing more dangerous than a woman scorned' haven't ever met an injured runner.

A thing I hate about running:

The freemium model of running. We have all seen the freemium model, such as the free app download or the sales funnel that gives you a free bit first. However, after the first taster there is always a payment option or an in-app purchase to be had.

Running is exactly like this. You can throw on some old shorts, trainers and leave the house in seconds. There you are, on the road or trail, free as a bird. But no sooner have you showered after that first taste than like a new drug, where the first hit was free, you now want more.

But by more, you mean new trainers, shorts, vest, base layers, special socks, Garmin, books, race fees, online coaching, physio, gait analysis... Before long, it's the most expensive sport known to man. The truth is, we don't run faster because of all this stuff, it just feeds our obsession.

Paul Hobrough is the author of The Runner's Expert Guide to Stretching: Prevent Injury, Build Strength and Enhance Performance.

Volunteer at a running event

One year, why not take the strain off your feet by volunteering at a local running event. You can become one of the heroes who make them happen. There are plenty of roles, from marshalling to tail-walking and handing out medals.

Run with principles

When parkrun announced it was to be sponsored by the controversial egg company HappyEggs, many people concerned with animal welfare vowed to boycott the event. It is worth investigating who is sponsoring your running event or how the running kit you make is manufactured. None of us can be perfect but we can all become more moral.

NUTRITION

Fuel is a runner's friend but getting running fuelling right can be a difficult challenge. How much pasta should you eat? What should you drink? How nutrition obsessed is the right level of nutrition obsessed and how nutrition obsessed is too nutrition obsessed?

It's not as easy as fuelling a car, is it? Find out more about running, eating and drinking, and how they relate to one another by devouring the pages ahead.

EAT RIGHT

The runner's body is an engine so it's vital you provide it with the very best fuel. What you drink and eat before, during and after your run will determine how enjoyable and successful your jogging life is.

Don't go full nutrition obsessive

If you've ever joined a running club or been a regular at the same parkrun, you will have met someone for whom watching what they eat and drink has become an obsession – a terrifying obsession.

Offset your treats

A great thing about running is that you can literally offset any food indulgences with mathematical precision. If you've eaten a 200-calorie cake, then simply add 3.2km (2 miles) to tomorrow's run.

Follow your tongue

Scientists at Loughborough University challenged runners to a 16km (10-mile) run under three refreshment conditions. One set were given nothing to drink, one were given drink at a prescribed schedule, and the third only drank when they felt thirsty. The third category ran most quickly. Proof that following your instinct rocks.

Put pasta in perspective

Pasta is something that runners have lost a bit of perspective about and has become a running cliché. For years, it was thought that eating a bowl of spaghetti the evening before a marathon would have such a transformational effect that it would jettison a mediocre, poorly prepared runner into a contender to win the damn thing.

The evening before big events, there would be 'pasta parties' at which participants could gather to chat and to load up on carbs. However, some runners would go crazy at these events. They would eat so much pasta that they would end up with a blood sugar crash, forcing their bodies to continue working to balance their blood sugar just when they needed a rest.

Some runners seem to think that carb loading is simply eating as much as possible for the two days before your event. Of course, this will only weigh you down and leave you feeling heavy and bloated on the big day, which is far from ideal. Others seem to think they should carb load for weeks on end before a marathon.

The fact is that many foods that are dense in carbohydrates also contain dietary fibre, which, while beneficial in small amounts, when eaten in large doses can lead to constipation and diarrhoea. Who needs a night of bloating, squitters and other forms of digestive discomfort before a big running event?

And yet this still happens among the less well-initiated and pasta mania has led many a runner to lose their grip. You can hear people lining up at parkrun discussing how they prepared for the run by carb loading in the days ahead. 'I starved myself of carbs on Tuesday and Wednesday and then totally overdosed on them on Thursday and Friday,' says one. 'Wow, you're totally going to get a PB today,' says their friend. All this for a 5K?

Pasta mania has even entered popular culture. In the US version of the sitcom *The Office*, the lead character Michael Scott announces proudly that he is 'carbo-loading' as he chows down on a huge serving of fettuccine alfredo just a few minutes before setting off on a charity run. Naturally, he throws up as he eventually arrives, exhausted, at the finishing line.

So can we all just wind it in a bit? Carb loading is a good plan, within reason, for longer-distance runs. However, if you are going to be out there for less than 90 minutes, it's simply unnecessary. For those runs where it is a benefit, it pays to approach it sensibly, consuming a wise amount of carbohydrates as part of a balanced intake. Even then, there is no need to limit yourself to pasta – there are many foods and drinks that will help you to obtain carbohydrates.

Stay hydrated all the time

Whether you are a runner or not, there are countless reasons to drink adequate, but not crazy amounts, of water every day. It can improve your mood, enhance your memory and reduce headaches. When you are more hydrated you will have fewer sugar cravings, plus it also prevents kidney stones, reduces the risk of bladder infections, gives you a brighter face and delays ageing. It lubricates the joints and delivers oxygen throughout the body, as well as flushing bodily waste.

For runners, there are additional reasons, since drinking plenty of water enhances exercise and helps you replace the fluids you lose through sweating. So, follow the *Code* and make sure you are always hydrated. Read on to work out how to do this.

Learn to spot the signs of dehydration

When you run, especially, but not only, on hot days, you risk dehydration, so it pays to learn the signs of it – such as dizziness, fatigue, cramps and nausea. A headache is another sign, as is urine that is dark. Aim for clear or straw-coloured pee.

Be sensible about sports drinks

That 1990s' John Barnes advert about isotonic drinks being 'in balance with your body fluids' has a lot to answer for. Until you are running 13km (8 miles) or more at a time, the main difference sports drinks will make will be to slap straight back on the calories you're trying to run off. So don't drink sports drinks for a 3.2km (2-mile) run. A glass of water will be fine.

Don't obsess over supplements

It all starts reasonably enough. The runner reads a few articles in running magazines about how much water to drink and what the correct ratios are for their carbs, their protein and their fat. Then they begin to read about superfoods and various vitamins and minerals. Hey, they're eating healthily. What is there to worry about?

Well, soon there will be things to worry about. As they pull up in their car at the event, it looks like they've done some sort of car-jacking at their local health food store. Rolling around the seats are bars and jars, powders and potions, even plastic mouth syringes. They neck mysterious pills on the starting line. At the finishing line, they start mixing hideous-looking green powder with coconut water. When you all go for your post-run coffee, they take their own weird brew, which includes butter.

Soon, they begin to cut a hyper, but spectral figure. Their cheek bones are forever on the brink of tearing through their face and they seem to always have too much or too little energy. They have basically forgotten that running is all about putting one foot in front of another quickly. They think it's all about what you eat and drink between runs.

Tom Usher

A thing I love about running: I can still
remember when I first read about the magical health
properties of green tea and was amazed. Four cups a day
and I'd burn fat and lose weight all on my own! Added to
some gym work and a relatively decent diet, it would get
me shredded in no time! Then I tried it, and although I'm
very aware the green tea I was and have been drinking
for about 10 years since is the most basic version, it
basically tastes like mud water. Hot, muddy water. But I've
bludgeoned myself over the head so much with its magical
health properties that I now believe it's nice, and drink it
repeatedly every day, even though I'm not even sure if I like
it, and in fact am pretty certain I hate it.

And what has that got to do with running? Well,
running is basically the green tea of the exercise world.
You see no immediate benefits: you don't get ripped, you
don't get hench and you don't look cool while you do it
(in fact you definitely look the opposite). And it sucks to
run, it's slow, long, painful and, if you're a heavy lad like
me, very uncomfortable on your knees. But for some
reason, I still do it nearly every morning, at least three
chugging, wheezing miles, that I'm not sure I'm enjoying
or benefitting from in any way, but just kind of do because
my brain has forced me at some kind of psychological
health gunpoint to keep doing it because it's good for me.
No you don't get it, I actually enjoy it! I 'love' running!
Seriously!

A thing I hate about running: What I hate about running, besides the fact that it is essentially just my brain holding me hostage to a vague notion of future health and physical prosperity, is how unexciting it is. With most other forms of exercise, be it sport, weights or miscellaneous (hiking or rock climbing or something like that), there is usually some form of active 'thrill' involved. Even golf, which is just professional walking, has a satisfying thwack sensation when you really tuck into a shot, and even hiking usually involves travelling through incredibly scenic locations. Running is just going round in a circle, usually just a few laps of the same park every time, often literally seeing the same runners go past you in the opposite, or worse, same direction as you. Even more brutal is being on a treadmill, which, to me, is as close to hell in terms of a boredom-to-constant-pain ratio as you can possibly get.

Tom Usher is a writer, presenter and all-round terrible runner.

Set a target for weight loss

If you want to lose weight to make you a better runner, it can be helpful to have a clear goal. This can work the same way as preparing for a long run on a specific date, and just as training is a gradual thing, so should weight loss be. A safe target for weight loss is 450g (1lb) a week.

Tailor your breakfast

What you should eat for breakfast on the day of a race depends on the length of that race. If it's a 5K, you could get away with a light meal or even no food at all. For a marathon, you'll need to load up.

Test meals during training

Make sure you test out any new meals during training for an event, rather than on the eve or day of the event itself. If that new meal is going to disagree with you it's better to find out on a training run than on the big day itself.

Remember your arteries

When I am eating any healthy food, I love to google its health benefits and read them as I eat. If you are ever struggling to keep going during a run, it can be nice to remind yourself of the benefits of running. So here's one for you: running unclogs your arteries.

Eat when you get home

You should eat within two hours of finishing a run, because this is the time when your muscles are best able to replenish their carbohydrate stores (glycogen). So even if the only thing you want to do is climb into the bath or crash on the sofa, head to the kitchen first, open your gob and shovel in plenty of healthy grub.

Don't drink and run

Running and boozing used to seem more separate than they do now. Obviously lots of runners drank, just as lots of drinkers ran. However, generally those who ran were doing so out of some sort of wider push for a healthier lifestyle. Therefore, big drinkers tended not to run many miles, and serious runners tended not to drink that much.

However, in recent years, the two pastimes have come closer together. For instance, more and more events have been launched that involve drinking alcohol and running at the same time. Events that would have seemed like something out of a comedy sketch show once upon a time have actually become real.

A truly French event, the Marathon du Médoc offers runners the chance to sample a selection of vinos at the 23 wine-tasting stations along the route. Well, it makes a change from boring old water, sports drinks and energy gels, I suppose. Participants are allowed up to 6 hours 30 minutes to complete the course. The condition they finish in rather depends on how enthusiastically they 'refuel'.

The Beer Lovers' Marathon is held in Liège, Belgium. As well as the familiar water and fuel stations, runners get to sample 15 different Belgian beers during the race. Prefer wine? On the Lanzarote Wine Run you can choose between taking on a half marathon or a 10km (6.2-mile) walk. Both go through Lanzarote's wine region, with wine tasting and tapas stops along the course.

This mixing of fitness and liquid indulgence is a growing thing. There are even gyms sponsored by booze companies, which combine working out and drinking. Anyway, assuming you're still here and you haven't dashed off to enter some boozy runs, I will continue.

There are of course reasons to be cautious about directly mixing alcohol with running. Remember that alcohol is both a poison and a diuretic, so it accelerates the dehydration process that running gives you at the best of times. Dehydration increases your risk for muscle cramps, muscle pulls, muscle strains and general fatigue increases. None of which is ideal.

However, research has been mixed on the issue. Some researchers have found that in moderation, a bit of sauce won't necessarily impair your performance. In one study, medics took 10 healthy individuals and gave them three shots of whisky before putting them on a treadmill to run to their maximum heart rate. Then, 48 hours later, they ran the same 10 subjects to exhaustion but without having served them whisky. The conclusion was that 'acute alcohol intake' is 'associated with a non-significant exercise performance reduction and stress hormone stimulation, with an unchanged exercise metabolism'.

There is even more good news for those of you who fancy blending your two favourite hobbies. Dr Matthew Barnes of New Zealand's Massey University says two drinks for men and one drink for women at least two hours before the event should be fine. He adds: 'More than that and you run the risk of dehydration and impaired judgement.'

This doesn't mean you should get smashed on the morning of your marathon but it does mean that, technically speaking at least, you can enjoy a drink and enjoy a run.

But should you run with a hangover?

No one likes a hangover. You don't need the *Code* to tell you that. The throbbing head, the nausea and the regret are not pleasant at all. The fact that these horrible symptoms are self-inflicted only adds to the nastiness because it mixes self-loathing into this vile cocktail. Add into the mix the fact that hangovers tend to get worse and longer as you get older, and you can understand why people become increasingly keen to shrug them off as quickly as possible.

Some people think a good run can do the trick. In years gone by, before scientists started poking their noses into sport, with their facts and their wisdom, people relied more on old wives' tales. One of these was that you could 'sweat out' a hangover with some good, hard exercise.

Therefore, many people concluded that running during a hangover was a doubly good idea: you got to 'sweat out' the alcohol by doing something worthy and healthy, and fit in your training. It all seemed a good idea.

However, there is no sporting scientific consensus on this. So stop before you stagger into you running shoes because experts say that the idea of 'sweating out' a hangover is a myth. All you end up doing is worsening one of the key causes of how rotten you feel: dehydration.

There are wider dangers, too. Running while hungover also puts you at higher risk of injuries: you are more likely to suffer muscle strains, cramps, muscle pulls and soreness, and electrolyte imbalances. You will be further straining your organs just when you don't need to.

Not only that, but you are much less likely to perform well if you run during a 'morning after'. Research by the American College of Sports Medicine found that everything from your aerobic power to your psychomotor skills are adversely affected by 'acute consumption of alcohol'. A separate study showed that consumption of a large amount of alcohol can reduce performance by up to 11.4 per cent.

So, all this points towards running while hungover being a bad idea. But then so was drinking too much the night before, so why would you listen to the *Code*? The same bravado that pushed you into overindulging can also push you into unwise behaviour the following morning. You wake up feeling terrible and tell yourself that a run would do you a lot of good. You think you can wipe out the hangover in a few easy miles.

If you do decide to do a run then hydrate as much as you can before you set out. Some experts suggest necking an anti-inflammatory, too. The process of detoxification places a lot of strain on your circulatory system, so it is more important than ever that you make sure you warm up properly before you set out. Also, this is not the time to set out on some epic distance or test some gruelling terrain. The *Code* says you should not run for more than 30 minutes, at a moderate tempo, if you are genuinely hungover. Keep your 20-milers, your hilly routes and your 6-minute miles for another day. In short: take it gently and rehydrate when you get home.

EVENTS

You know what a lot of runners missed during the pandemic? Events. In all but the strictest lockdowns, we were still allowed to get out and run. Many of us actually ran more than usual, as our hobby helped us feel free during the era of restriction. But these solo runs couldn't replace the excitement and sense of achievement that we get from events.

People talk about the 'loneliness' of the runner but we're not always alone. Whether it is a small local parkrun or globally famous events like the London or New York marathons, these events bring much-needed excitement and solidarity to the running family.

As running events mercifully start up again, the *Code* has tips for how to make the most of them as a participant. So read on and discover water station etiquette, best practice for toilets and how to finish.

A thing I love about running: The one thing I love about running is how it brings people together, whether it be online or in real life. It connects people from all walks of life, backgrounds, cultures and faiths. Running binds us and is a commonality that allows us to meet people we may never have done otherwise.

A thing I hate about running: The amount of extra clothes I have to end up washing and ironing ... and that's all I have to say on that!

Tazneem Anwar blogs at **This Hijabi Runs.**

YOUR PRE-EVENT CHECKLIST

You've spent months training for a big event. How you spend the days before the starting pistol sounds will have a big influence on how successful and enjoyable the run is. Lots of running advice tells you what not to do at this stage, but what about the things you should do?

Sleep well

There's some good news here for those who get anxious the evening before a race. Researchers have found that the most important sleep is the one *two* nights before a race. So get a good kip on that night and don't worry too much if your sleep is disturbed the following evening.

Plan your route

No, not the route of the event itself – the route to the starting line of the event. You won't want any tension or confusion on the morning of the run, so get yourself clear on where you're going and how you'll get there. Bear in mind that there might be road closures on the big day.

Trim your toenails carefully

If your toenails are particularly long then you might like to give them a trim. But clip them carefully; if you are overzealous about this you can cause soreness, right when you don't want it. Also, *see* 'Dispose of toenail clippings' on p. 36.

Drink plenty of water

Obviously. But not too much. *See* p. 161.

Plan something relaxing

It could be nice to watch a favourite, trusted film to help you stay calm and relaxed the night before the big run.

Pack your bag early

A bottle of water, some emergency cash, clothing to warm you up.

Don't complain about entry fees

Arranging a major running event can be a very complex and costly undertaking so try not to complain about the entry fees. Running is still a very cheap sport and you are under no obligation to enter any events. So if you choose to, don't be one of those runners who struts around near the finishing line, saying: 'Forty quid? FORTY QUID?'

Don't freshen up in public

At the start of running events there's often that guy who starts applying anti-chafing lube to his more personal regions, right there in front of everyone. If you don't spot him there, don't worry, because you will easily find him at the finish. He'll be the one who took his top off and started spraying deodorant. These people are awful.

Always go to the loo before you set out

Ever been caught short during a run? You're not alone: the jostling motion can cause muscle contractions in the intestines, moving whatever you have eaten along the chain. The simple answer is to always pop into the loo before you set out for a run. I feel like the *Code* is talking quite a bit about matters lavatorial but it is important to get these things right.

Treat the toilets like they're in your home

The state of the toilets at running events is not something we need to go into gory detail about here. If you've seen them, you'll know what I'm on about. If you haven't, well, lucky you. The *Code* begs you – please treat portaloos with the same respect you would the toilet in your own home.

Train as closely as you can for the event

Does the event you're training for have lots of hills? Yes? Include some hilly routes during your training. Does it have an early morning start time? Do as much of your training as you can in the early morning. Are you aiming for a specific finish time on the day? Train at the appropriate pace.

Don't do the tourist trail the day before a big event

The last thing you need the day before running 42km (26.2 miles) is a day on your feet, with physical exertion and mental stimulation galore. Take it easy instead. You can always hobble round the sights the following day.

Check the final section of the course

Before you run in an event, it's a good idea if possible to lightly jog along the final section of the course, to find a landmark from which you can speed up for a faster finish.

Be prepared to adjust your goals

If on the big day there are strong winds, sapping heat, torrential rain or other weather horrors then be open to adjusting your plans for pace and finish time. It's better to enjoy the day by approaching the course realistically than trying to hang on to a plan that was made with easier conditions in mind. You can aim for that target on a more clement day. For today, just run for the reality you have found yourself in.

Treat expos like bank robberies

The very last thing your body needs on the eve of a marathon is to spend ages around loads of strangers at a running expo. Your immune system may be a bit on the low side if you've spent months training for a marathon. The same is probably true of your fellow runners. The last thing any of you need is to be swapping germs. So if you have to go to the expo because it's the only way you can get your number bib, make sure you get in and out quickly. Basically, treat it like you would a bank raid.

Don't diss short distances

When some runners start tackling half marathons and marathons they become snotty about shorter running events. When another runner tells them they are training for a 5K or 10K, this sort of runner snorts with derision and wonders aloud whether such distances are 'really worth it'. These people are wallies. Don't be a wally.

Don't call a marathon a 'full'

Yes, there are half marathons and full marathons. It's OK to call a half marathon a 'half' but please don't call a full marathon a 'full'. It just sounds weird.

Don't obsess about marathons

For many runners, one of the greatest pleasures of the pursuit is its autonomy. In a world where our career and family can put all sorts of demands and pressures on to our shoulders, it's lovely to have a regular part of our lives that we are in control of. We can run as much or as little as we want. We can choose our own routes. We can decide how seriously to take it and how important it is to us.

But one thing sometimes gets in the way of this: the marathon. A lot of people get into running because they want to run a marathon. We are brought up with a big 26-miler as part of our nation's calendar, so it's natural that when we think about taking up running, it is the marathon that seems the obvious target to aim at.

Every spring there is the London Marathon and then in November there is the New York Marathon. Most cities have them: there are an estimated 800 major marathon events each year. They are the challenges that are dangled in front of us and that become, rightly or wrongly, the flagship distance for any runner.

While running a marathon is a wonderful challenge and an experience you will remember for the rest of your life, it is not the be-all and end-all of running. No runner should feel obliged to take part in one. You can set yourself time challenges and run 5Ks, or even go all-out for endurance running events, with distances that dwarf the mere 42km (26.2 miles) of marathons.

For a lot of runners, the half marathon is a good fit: it provides a challenging distance but not one that makes training dominate your life for months beforehand, nor one that cripples you on the day.

And let's not overlook the good, honest wholesomeness of 10Ks. For many runners, this was the first challenging event we entered. It's easy to forget what a big deal it once was for us to complete 10km (6.2 miles) without stopping. It can be nice to return to that challenge.

Then there are the 'curious' runs, which are becoming more of a feature of the running calendar. Muddy runs and other obstacle events are another option for relatively new or experienced runners to aim at. Go curveball on us!

Whatever you choose, don't feel that you have to run a marathon to be a runner. Some runners can make you feel this way as they brag about the marathons they've run. Non-runners, too, can make you feel you are not a real runner until you've done the big one.

Since running is a generally solitary pursuit, you should approach it the way *you* want to. It can become the part of your life where you call all the shots and set your own goals.

And if running a marathon is not one of your goals, just ignore anyone who makes you feel it should be. Run your way and no one else's. It's the only way to do it.

GUEST FEATURE   *Martin Melly*

A thing I love about running: The freedom it gives me – both physically and mentally. When I set off and get into a rhythm it's just the road and me, I'm alone with my thoughts and I'm only going up against myself. This is one of my favourite things in life. When I'm running, my imagination runs free, too. I can be anything I want to be. I believe in myself and begin to solve problems and think clearly about how I want to approach things and get my thoughts in order. It clears my head and allows me to build confidence to take on things I was maybe apprehensive about. I don't often feel like that, like I could take on anything, but running gives me that belief.

A thing I hate about running: Simply that I am not better at it. I know I am usually only competing against myself but I always want to do better and there are so many wee factors that can impact on your run. Weather, slight injuries, fatigue all play a part and it would be impossible to run faster or beat your previous personal best every time you set off. But that still can be frustrating. The key is to keep going back for more and like most things in life, never give up.

Martin Melly is a runner from Glasgow and one of the hosts of the Celtic podcast @20MinuteTims. Follow him on Twitter at @martinmelly86.

Double-knot your laces at the starting line

There is nothing worse for you than realising early on in a race that your shoelaces have come undone. So make sure they are tied firmly before the starting pistol is fired, otherwise they'll keep coming undone every couple of hundred metres and when you suddenly stop to re-tie them other runners will fall over you. And I've found people don't take well to that.

Take the eve of a race seriously ... but not too seriously

The day before a long race it is important to prepare well for the big event. There are obvious things to do, such as eating the right foods, hydrating well and not doing anything strenuous. It's probably not the day to do intensive gardening or to head out to the pub. You've spent many months getting ready for the big day, so it would be awful to waste all that effort and time by messing up the final 24 hours.

You can take your lead from the pros in any sports on this. Some professional cyclists have a rule for the day before a big race: don't sit when you can lie, and don't stand when you can sit. They will even wait for a lift in order to go up one floor, when they would usually take the stairs. Footballers famously sometimes avoid sex for a day or two before a match. (Or so they say.)

You really don't need to go that far but it is worth avoiding any situation that will tire you or stress you out. Sometimes, these deviations come unexpectedly. I once prepared particularly carefully for a half marathon. For months, I trained harder and more attentively, hoping to get a PB on the big day.

The day before, I successfully took it easy until I took my dog, Harry, for a walk in a big field. My thinking was that he could happily stretch his legs in the field while I sat and watched. He got exercise but my legs were spared.

It worked well until Harry spotted a young deer and immediately took off to chase it. Given that the far end of the field backs on to a motorway, I had to run after Harry to try to prevent either him or the deer running out there. Both animals were faster than I expected, so it turned into a prolonged and exhausting sprint.

I probably broke all manner of speed records in that field but the next day at the event itself I was nowhere near a PB and even managed to almost collapse with cramp in the final mile. Harry is the sort of disaster you cannot legislate for, but do what you can. Take the day before a run seriously and much of the run will take care of itself.

All of this said, it is also important to not take the race or yourself *too* seriously. Partners of runners are likely to roll their eyes if, on the eve of a 10K, their loved one is acting as if the following day they are taking part in a globally-televised Ironman Triathlon, or a marathon that finishes at the tip of Mount Everest.

There is a balance to be struck between sensible preparation and wild lack of self-awareness. You know in your heart where that balance lies. Prepare well, but not too well.

DOS AND DON'TS DURING THE EVENT

When you turn up to a big running event it can feel like your first day at school. There are strangers everywhere and they're all a bit wired and nervous. Here's how to navigate the day, including what to wear, how to be kind and why it's important not to bend the rules.

Be welcoming ... but not too welcoming

If you run any sort of regular running event it's nice when you're welcoming to newcomers. But don't be so welcoming that they start wondering if they need a restraining order.

Don't wave if you don't want to

Although it can be nice to greet another runner during an everyday run (*see* p. 57), you shouldn't feel you have to wave to every spectator at a running event. Frankly, those spectators who demand to be greeted as you run past them are a proper pest. Don't even think of succumbing to their demand that you wave as you run past, you will only encourage them.

Don't think your finish time is still heroic

I remember when a sub-4-hour marathon was, like, woooaaaaah! Now, it's all about sub-3-hour finish times. It feels like every 10 years the impressive PB for any distance is revised. So, if your PB is from several years ago, make sure it's still impressive before you boast to the cool kids.

Organising an event? Start it on time

IF YOU'VE RUN a few 10Ks or half marathons, or if you've got some parkruns under your running belt, you will probably have endured a delayed start. These are the athletic equivalent of the delayed flight and can be just as frustrating.

You've pumped yourself up for a specific start time. You've made the effort to ensure you arrive at the park on time. Your intake of food, liquid and any supplements has all been scheduled for that specific start time. Indeed, every part of your warm-up, including pre-run stretching, has been timed carefully.

So it's a real shame when you find yourself standing at the starting line or in a cramped starting funnel as a delay sets back the start time. When you want to be running free, you are instead stuck amid your fellow runners. In this sea of Lycra, you can only hear squeaking running apps and frustrated 'tuts'. This wasn't what you spent all those months preparing for.

Sometimes, these delays are unavoidable and out of the hands of the organisers. It may be that the start has been postponed for the safety of the runners. This is all well and good and completely understood, but there are times when the delay is unnecessary. Parkrun is a regular offender for this. When the run marshals give their pre-run briefing, some of them seem to forget that the word 'briefing' includes the word *brief*. Before you know it, they've not just given you the rundown on the event but also the very history of athleticism itself and a handful of in-jokes just to pad it out a bit more. All as you stand there, visibly

▷

frustrated as the 9 a.m. start time is pushed back further and further.

I also ran at a longer-distance event when the start time was delayed by 20 minutes because the organiser suspected a few runners may have been held up in traffic. Suspected! Likewise at a 10K, we were held up for 25 minutes at the start. No explanation was given but then the run suddenly started once a celebrity runner had arrived at the starting line. Hmmm.

Putting aside unavoidable delays, the *Code* would like to encourage event organisers to put a lot of effort into getting the runs started on time. It's a key part of an enjoyable and successful event. Don't leave us hanging!

What if ...
you get attacked by insects?

During the warmer months, insects can really earn their 'pests' name tag. One minute, you're running along, enjoying the bliss of summer. The next, you have an insect flying up your nose.

Well, that insect must have had a lover that was missing it because, two minutes later, another bug flies into your mouth. Later in the run, a third insect flies into your eyes. They're such little rotters!

Each time you're attacked by an insect you will want to get rid of it as quickly as possible but make sure you step away from the trail to do this. No one wants to see a runner firing snot out of their beak. Equally, if you start wretching as you try to cough up an insect, you might worry passers-by.

There are also ways to reduce your chances of being bugged by bugs in the first place:

- Wear sunglasses – that's your eyes protected.
- Don't run with your mouth wide open – you're not Napoleon Dynamite.
- Wear insect repellent.
- Avoid running past ponds and lakes because insects collect there.
- Don't wear blue – while designing fly traps, researchers from the University of Florida found that flies are attracted to blue and repelled by yellow.

Don't eat or drink anything new, or wear new kit, on race day

One year, as I lined up at the start of the Windsor Half Marathon, I cringed as the guy next to me proudly told me that he was wearing a brand-new, box-fresh pair of trainers for the special day. 'In fact,' he continued with a big smile, 'all of my kit is brand new. I bought it all especially for the run.'

I wished him well and I hope he had a great run but his was a very bad approach. He ran the risk of blisters from the new trainers and chafes from the fresh kit. It is not freshness but familiarity that you should aim for on the big day.

Sometimes at the expo on the eve of the run you are given a technical T-shirt and some carb gel in your goodie bag. It can be tempting to don the shirt and neck the gel for the run. Tempting but mistaken. Similarly, if you're staying in a hotel for the marathon, you might be tempted to try something new for breakfast on the big day. But this isn't the time to find out that bagels with cream cheese give you the trots.

At the run itself, don't decide on a whim to run alongside a pacer. If during your training you haven't maintained a fast pace then it's going to give your body a heck of a shock to suddenly do it at the event. It's most likely that you will exhaust yourself in the opening miles and then be playing catch-up for the rest of the route.

So make sure you don't try anything new on race day. No new kit, no new drinks or gels, no new stretches. You don't want to discover the hard way that those trainers give you blisters or that that gel makes you projectile vomit. Stick with the old trusties and have a nice run.

Stay aware and keep your distance

When runners are packed together in a narrow part of a course it only takes one runner to fall over or switch off mentally to cause the runner behind them to also be in trouble. Before you know it, runners are knocking into each other, slipping over and being whacked off their pace. Skinny limbs and recriminations fill the air.

These issues are often more common in the final section of the course. People start running faster, their minds and bodies are tired and their thoughts for those around them are clouded by thoughts of a faster arrival at the finishing line.

Runners can learn from the experience of cyclists. The reason those Tour de France pile-ups are so messy is that the cyclists speed along so tightly packed. Sardines would get claustrophobic in those pelotons. It only takes one tiny issue for the whole affair to come crashing to the pavement.

Nobody wants scenes like that at running events. The first thing you can do is keep a safe distance from your fellow runners. That way, if one of them falls, you will be able to avoid joining them on the pavement. See it as an athletic version of the chevrons rule in driving.

Second, just stay aware. Lots of us can go into a hypnotic state during runs and we can also be distracted by the music or chatter coming through our headphones. But you have a responsibility to yourself and to those around you to stay aware enough to avoid causing a pile-up. Run as you would if you were driving down a road.

GUEST FEATURE | *Nicky Campbell*

A thing I love about running: I love letting go. But never with music. I don't want to be hamstrung by Dylan or Drake. Only my own thoughts for what they're worth for some times when they are worth it. They can break a mental logjam, light a creative fuse or merely take me from less than zero to four out of 10. And four – well that's sometimes enough. Sometimes that's like climbing Everest. I love the hard, lung-busting, sweet-sweat-dripping effort and all while sightseeing. I love being overtaken by people I once left in my wake and thinking good for them but I want to catch them up and say 'Big deal City boy. Suck on this – I'm nearly 60.' But clearly I never reached maturity. I love getting home.

A thing I hate about running: The knees are my downfall. I am limited to 5km (3 miles) twice a week, if that. I look at the watch and I've become the guy delighted to break a 9-minute mile. A 10-minute mile. Call it 11 but this is unbearable to write. Once it was 6. I can't look at the watch too much. That timepiece is an intimation of mortality. That timepiece waits for no man. And neither does the flash City boy fecker. But one day his knees will be his nemesis, too.

Nicky Campbell is one of Britain's most distinguished broadcasters. Over the past four decades he has presented Wheel of Fortune, Watchdog, Long Lost Family *and* Big Questions.

Follow water station etiquette

Water stations are a godsend at running events. It's easy to take them for granted but stop and think about it for a moment: people stand there for hours on end, handing out water to sweaty, grunting strangers. Doesn't that warm your heart?

It's important to value water stations and to make the most of them. Here's how:

- First, hydrate yourself properly before a race. Sometimes water stations get too crowded to stop at, or they can run out of water, so the less dependent you are on them, the better.
- Don't stop abruptly. The runner behind you might not be intending to use this water station, so if you suddenly halt, you could cause a collision. Check behind you before you pull over. (Actually, that applies to when you stop for any reason over the whole course.)
- If there is a row of tables, don't stop at the first one. This will only make a pile-up of thirsty runners more likely – and no one wants a pile-up of thirsty

runners. If there is just one table, stop at the furthest point along it. There will be more room and you'll cause less congestion.

- Thank the volunteers.
- When you go to grab a cup, try to make eye contact with the volunteer. If you don't have eye contact with them, it's quite likely that they will be looking at another runner, whom they intend to hand the cup to.
- Thank the volunteers. Always thank the volunteers.
- Don't take more than one cup of water unless you are certain that it's OK to.
- Don't be grumpy if the handover isn't smooth enough to mean you don't need to slow down for it. Nobody is forcing you to stop at all.
- Once you have your cup or bottle, get the hell out of the water station area. The idea isn't that you stand there, propping up the bar and sharing small talk with the volunteers, or trying to chat them up. Get out!
- Feel free to pour the water over your head. It's your water and you're free to do what you like with it. But make sure you are actually throwing it on *your* head. It's easy to be overexcited about the process and end up chucking it backwards, into the face of the runner behind you.
- Also, don't dramatically shake the water from your hair, as if you're a supermodel emerging from a hotel pool, or just some berk in a shampoo advert. Nobody wants to be sprayed by your sweat-laced water, even on a hot day.

- Use the bins if there are bins. If not, throw your cup or bottle to the side of the course (so others don't slip on them) and as near to the tables as possible (so it's easier to gather them up afterwards).
- The same goes if you are combining a gel wrapper with your water. (Or, even better, stash the empty wrapper in your shorts pocket or running belt).
- A safety tip: if the water station provides bottles rather than cups, don't replace the lid before you dispose of them, because if you run over an empty bottle without a lid it should just crumple, whereas a bottle with the lid on can cause a nasty slip.
- Watch for runners behind you before you throw your cup or bottle to the side of the course. Someone might be coming up fast on your left and right, and they won't want your disposed vessel in their face.
- If you are spectating at a race and you see that the water station volunteers are struggling to keep on top of things then go and offer some help. Even 20 minutes could make the world of difference.
- If you see a runner, or volunteer, handling the handover in a way you find less than ideal, feel free not to share your feelings with them. Handing over water during a hectic running event is stressful enough as it is.
- Oh, and did I say that you should always thank the volunteers?

Don't cut corners

Have you even existed unless a parent or teacher has told you that 'you're only letting yourself down' during a childhood rollicking? Well, I'm about to be that rollicker.

If you cut corners during a run, you certainly are letting yourself down. What use is it to shave five seconds off your parkrun personal best if you know that you didn't really run the full 5km (3 miles)? When you close your eyes at night, how do you feel about that tainted achievement? How would you explain it to your dog, who idolises you? Honestly, you're so naughty!

However, I cannot rock out the 'only letting yourself down' cliché here because you are also letting down your fellow runners. I recall with horror the awkward parkrun briefing where the run director told the assembled masses that he had noticed some people cutting corners the previous week. We all looked at each other accusingly and the atmosphere became a toxic blend of recrimination and guilt.

And well may the offenders have felt guilty – for those parkrunners who aim for an impressive finishing position it was disheartening to discover that some of their fellow dashers had been cutting corners. It was also an awkward moment: why would any grown adult turn up to a fun event like parkrun and cheat?

Well, in one case, it was a professional motivation. *Runner's World* magazine sent along a journalist to attend a parkrun to secretly 'cheat' by not completing the full 5km (3 miles), and then write about his experience. He might have been letting himself down but at least he wasn't letting his editor down, I guess. For the rest of us, though, there is no excuse. Stop cutting corners.

Don't set out too hard

The excitement and adrenaline of a big running event can easily conspire to make you set out too fast. You are at the peak of your months of training and all pumped up. You want to make a success of it. When the starting pistol is fired, you are out of the traps as if you are running a 100m race rather than 16km (10 miles). You will pay for that big start all the way round the course. Start well and you will finish well.

HOW TO FINISH

Finishing a running event with dignity and consideration is such a challenge that getting it right is almost a work of art. After all, you are tired and pumped up, so it is easy to lose your tethering. Here's how to do it right.

Don't suddenly stop

Sure, you've finished the course and it feels great. It's quite a moment. But if you suddenly stop at the finishing line or in the finishers' funnel, you're going to ruin that moment for other people.

When you stop dead in your tracks the person behind you will need to stop dead in their tracks and before you know it, you've created a motorway-style pile-up. This is at best annoying and at worst dangerous for your fellow runners.

So rather than stopping dead, why not slow down and stroll along until you are away from the finishing line itself. Be aware of what is going on around you.

Don't rub it in

Sometimes runners like to carry on jogging after they've crossed the finishing line. A particular example of this is the early finisher who dons his medal and then trots effortlessly along the side of the final section of the route, silently shaming the runners who are still breathlessly completing the course.

Others have been known to go even further. There should be a special place in hell for the runner who passes the finishing line, drops to the ground and pumps out 20 press-ups, as other runners collapse around him. Oh do sod off!

Be nice to volunteers

If marshals hand you a drink, medal or T-shirt, make sure you thank them.

Congratulate other runners

This might be the umpteenth half marathon you have run but there is a good chance that the person finishing alongside you might have completed the distance for the first time. This might be one of the most exciting and fulfilling moments of their lives. So give everyone some love.

Be gracious

If you find yourself approaching the finishing line of a parkrun or other running event alongside another runner, you don't need to turn it into some sort of challenge to see which of you will finish first. Unless you know that they'd appreciate a sprint challenge, why not just let them finish first.

The day after a big run

THE AFTERMATH OF a long run can be as memorable as the day itself. Here's what to expect.

Stiff or wobbly legs

The further you ran the day before, the more weird your legs will feel. Sometimes you will wander around so stiffly you look more like a metal frame than a human being. Or, your legs might be trembling. Either way, the correct way to respond is with a sort of heroic stoicism.

Chafing

You won't be able to forget you've just run a half marathon because all day, the top of your inner thighs will remind you.

Interacting with family

'The third mile was big, I really think it was there that I set up the PB. Oh, and I didn't mention this that happened in mile 18...' What lucky relatives they are.

Planning your next run

Your friends and family have become bored of how much running has come to dominate your life and your conversation. Just when they thought you'd got it out of your system by running that marathon, you fill in the entry form for your next one.

A thing I love about running: The sense of pure freedom and an ability to get off the beaten track – to places where cars and bikes can't go. When you're having a good run and hit a rhythm and transcend, the hours just whizz by, it's like moving meditation – so good for the soul!

A thing I hate about running: The sausage runs. You know, the days when you feel like a sausage on legs. Entirely unbuilt for purpose. Heavy. Lethargic. When every mile feels like it takes an hour. Those days come out of nowhere and always catch me by surprise.

Anna McNuff is the author of The Pants of Perspective.

CLEVER RUNNING

U p there for thinking and down there for dancing, they say. Well, sometimes mind and body can work in tandem. If you want to become a better runner you'll need to work on your body but you'll also need to sharpen up your mind. Here, the *Code* shows you how to run smarter and get the edge.

LEARN FROM THE EXPERTS

As runners, we are not standing on the shoulders of giants so much as running in the wake of many who have trodden the path before us. There's an abundance of wisdom out there for any of us willing to keep our eyes and ears open, in our endless quest to run better.

Watch other runners

One of the most educational and enjoyable parkruns I ever experienced was one that I didn't take part in. One week, I went along to study other runners. I noticed that the very fastest runners had 'resting face' even as they powered along. There was not even the hint of a grimace. Had you snapped a photo of their faces as they sped along, you could have used the images for passports.

Other things I noticed: those who finished at the front frequently went over the finishing line with snot and saliva happily sliding down their faces. From this, I took that even wiping such nastiness away was considered an unnecessary distraction during the run.

I also learned a whole load more – about gaits, breathing and more. I therefore recommend that you watch other runners more. You'll be surprised how much you discover.

Be honest when you ask for advice

As a beginner, it can be tempting to inflate your achievements when you're speaking to more experienced runners. But whether you are asking a fellow runner for tips, or shopping for shoes in a specialist running shop, the more accurate a picture you paint of where you stand, the better their help will be.

Try visualisation

If you want to get a PB at a running event then you can try visualisation to help you reach your goal. Picture yourself running quickly and effortlessly. If you are familiar with the course you will be running, make the picture in your head as vivid as you can, with landmark details. Imagine you are nailing that finishing time you wanted.

Don't change everything at once

Are you planning to add swimming or weight training to your weekly exercise schedule? Great, but then that week won't be the one in which you also increase your mileage. Likewise, if you are adding a hilly course to your schedule then that won't be the day, or even the week, to also try to drastically speed up your pace.

Run to the hills

Don't worry, I'm not going to get all Iron Maiden on you. (Although the heavy metal band's song 'Run to the Hills' is a cracker of a track to listen to while you're out for a run. Particularly if you're running on hilly terrain.) I am simply here to point out that there are so many benefits to running up and down hills. Hilly running will improve your dynamic power, hip strength and hip mobility. Why? Because you need to be able to go and drive those hips really high to get up.

Running up hills is also great for your endurance because it requires both your heart and your head to run harder. That sense of challenge of running uphill is matched by the sense of achievement when you reach the top.

It enhances your leg-muscle strength, boosts your cardiovascular system and tones up your backside. (Don't pretend you didn't perk up when that last benefit was mentioned.) Hills can also improve your running form because they encourage you to swing your arms properly, a part of everyday running form that many of us ignore.

Finally, they will stand you in good stead for any running events. Many event courses include a hill or two and you will feel fantastic if you are one of the runners who dashes up them without any difficulty, rather than one of the runners who groan and gives up on the slopes. And just think what that will do for your finishing time!

So get out there, run to the foot of the hill, and take a deep breath. And yes, when you get to the top of a hill, feel free to stop and roar, like someone from some sort of Sylvester Stallone film. It's not just acceptable, it's more or less compulsory.

GUEST FEATURE | *Rachel Cullen*

A thing I love about running: Answer: freedom. For those 30, 60, 90 – whatever – minutes, the rest of the world can jog on. I don't care what's trending on Twitter; my daughter can't holler at me from upstairs because she wants me to fetch her an iPhone charger that she could easily get for herself. I'm not looking at a dishwasher waiting to be unpacked or wondering how much longer I can go without changing the beds. Running consumes me. I am outdoors and I am free. I have the other handy distractions of occasionally thinking about my pacing, my heart rate or my route, but they are the only things on my radar. The rest of the world can wait.

A thing I hate about running: The fact that doing hill reps supposedly 'gets easier' when it never actually feels any easier. They make me want to vomit. Every single time.

Rachel Ann Cullen is the author of Running for my Life: How I built a better me one step at a time.

Treat yourself

Reached your monthly mileage target? Nailed a tricky pace? Completed a previously unimaginable distance? You could be all sensible and grown-up and consider the achievement to be a reward in itself. But who wants to be all sensible and grown-up all the time? The *Code* says that you can afford to double up the reward by treating yourself. So get yourself an indulgent snack, use your favourite oil in the bath or buy yourself a little running-related gift.

You're more likely to complete your next big target if you associate it with a treat. So when you've done well, hit the shops or get those confirmation emails landing in your inbox.

Having a great run? Don't extend it

Some days, everything just feels great as you run. The run feels effortless and both your body and mind are buzzing. Don't be tempted to add extra miles to your planned distance. Going in on a high is much better for your future attitude to running than ruining a successful run by stretching it out.

Run against the traffic

The best way to avoid crashing into a vehicle is to be able to see them and the best way to be able to see vehicles is to run against the traffic. Don't expect drivers and cyclists to be your best friends, though. Plenty of them act like territorial dogs the moment they see a runner anywhere near the curb. And if you haven't had a car drive through a puddle and splash you then you're not putting enough miles in.

Don't expect to like every runner

When you arrive at a social event or start a job at a new workplace you are sometimes introduced to another runner. People assume that the fact that you and another human being both go out and pound the pavements will mean you are bound to get along and become, like, the best friends ever. You're guaranteed to hit it off!

This is often a rather presumptuous and optimistic view. People who share the same religion often don't get along all that well, so why should two runners like one another? Members of the same political parties often fight like angry cats, so why would joggers be instant best mates? Even fans of the same football team can be at each other's throats. I mean, have you ever looked at Twitter?

You could point to the fact that runners are likely to see the world the same way, to have the same mindset. But even if this were true, consider what sort of mindset runners have: one that enjoys running away from other people and spending hours every week on their own. It hardly sounds like the sort of recipe for friendship.

Just as lots of runners enjoy their alone time, lots of us are competitive, too. If we are proud of our personal best at 5K or of how many marathons we've run, it's not going to feel great if we meet another runner who is more accomplished than us. After all, in any conversation between two runners, one of them is going to be the person who has run faster and longer. This can really sting.

I remember chatting to another runner about the Windsor Half Marathon, which we had both participated in the previous year. He asked me how I had got on. 'I finished in 1 hour 52 minutes,' I told him, proudly, and asked him how he had got on. 'Oh, I came third,' he replied. Well, that put me in my place.

Equally, at your local running club or parkrun there are bound to be characters who you don't enjoy. Us runners are a curious bunch. The sort of people who forego a lie-in on a winter's morning in favour of huffing round a freezing park before sunrise or who train for a year for a run so long that it makes our nipples bleed are likely to be eccentric characters who might rub up one another, like our nipples, the wrong way at the best of times.

That said, many runners have made great friends and found the love of their life through running. Many derive a sense of community and fun from running clubs and parkruns. It is being among other runners that makes the experience so special for them. This is great.

But you know what? Not all of us are like that and if you don't get along with every runner you come across, then that doesn't mean there's anything wrong with you. Runners are a curious and varied bunch. You can't like all of us.

GUEST FEATURE | *Leanne Davies*

A thing I love about running: For me, what I really love about running is the social side of it. Running has brought so many amazing friends into my life that I can't imagine being without now. Running has also given me a huge deal of confidence in myself that I didn't have before. As a mum, I think running sets a great example to my two boys about the importance of exercise, for both physical and mental health.

> *A thing I hate about running:* There's not much
> I hate about running! I guess that now I feel hopelessly
> addicted to it, to the point where if I don't run (through
> injury or lack of time), my frame of mind can suffer a little.
> I guess that just means I will have to keep running in my
> life forever!
>
> *Leanne Davies is the co-author of* Run Mummy Run: Inspiring
> Women to Be Fit, Healthy and Happy.

Cyclists aren't your friends

You might imagine, mightn't you, that runners and cyclists may be members of some sort of coalition of solidarity. A Venn diagram of fitness that highlights what we have in common, rather than what differentiates us. But remember you're talking about *cyclists*, those perennially indignant people who don't seem to like anyone any more. So why would they like runners?

Vary your routes

A change is as good as a rest, they say, and running can very much prove this. If you hit a slump in your running and start to feel unmotivated, it's easy to ignore what the obvious and simple cause could be. It could be the very ground you are treading upon.

If you are running the same route, week in, week out, after a while, there's a good chance you will start to grow bored of it. The same old lamp posts, that part of the park where the terrain gets a bit gravelly and that bloke with his dog who always seems to appear at the same point.

For a long time, these milestones can be positives. The familiarity of the route can help keep a steady rhythm to your training. As you pass each of them, you feel at home and safe in your run. But after a while, they can begin to hinder you. Thought patterns can become repetitive because you anchor certain landmarks across the route with particular topics in your mind.

Eventually, the entire experience becomes like a scene from *Groundhog Day*. Everything is just too predictable. So it's little wonder that you start to make excuses not to get out there and run. Like a student who starts to do ironing, or clean their bedroom, or do almost anything rather than start writing that essay, the bored runner will start doing DIY tasks or catching up on emails to avoid running. They might even imagine twinges and injuries they don't really have.

Yet it's often the case that all they needed to do was to try a new running route. Move from the park to the riverside, or run along roads in a different direction from your home, or even travel to a new area for a run. You may be surprised by the rush of motivation this gives you.

The same goes for running events. If you are struggling to grab a PB at your local parkrun, have you tried travelling to one in a different area? The adrenalin of the new surroundings and people can make you run that bit harder and faster, powering you to a new PB. Even if you don't run the route faster, you will find it more exciting and interesting than a parkrun route you've run dozens of times before.

While you are changing your regular training routes, you might consider some more tweaks to your running experience. Sometimes, changing what you listen to can freshen things up.

If you've been listening to podcasts for a while, maybe switch to music. Or leave the headphones at home and listen to the sounds of the world? A bit of new kit can also give you a boost and so can running at a different time of day.

None of this advice is to dismiss how demoralising and difficult it can be when you lose your running motivation. I should know, as it has happened to me. After more than a decade of always running in the mornings, I once reached a point where I was no longer interested in running any more.

This is a source of widespread terror among runners: the fear that one day you will just lose, irretrievably, your running mojo. You will become an ex-runner, slouching broadly in front of the television, rather than dashing lithely along in the open air. You will end up overweight and depressed. You'll get out of breath walking up just one flight of stairs. In short, you will become that archetypal fat guy you've always sneered secretly at.

All these thoughts and more went through my mind as I lost my running momentum. I started to get out there less and less. My weekly mileage grew smaller and smaller. Then it hit the dreaded zero. I struggled for several weird months to get back into it.

A curious and frustrating dichotomy was holding me back: I dearly wanted to run, but something stopped me. The desire was there but the motivation vanished. It was like I was pushing and pulling on my front door. From a man who gleefully ran marathons, I became a mouse who could not psych himself up for a mere jog around the local park.

And I did indeed start to put on weight. At first, I thought I was merely being vain and paranoid. However, when women over the age of 60 began to compliment me on how well I was looking, I realised I must be getting fat. (Let's be real: 'looking well' in old ladies' speak always means 'looking plump'.)

A more direct verdict came when I took my lovely niece Verity swimming. As I emerged from my changing cubicle she looked at me and said: 'Oh, you've ... changed.'

Ouch! Well, at least my horror over it all forced me to acknowledge how important weight loss had been to my passion for running. When non-exercisers would marvel at how I kept off the pounds through my jogging, I'd brush the matter aside. 'No no, that's not what it's about,' I'd protest. But as I lost my running mojo, I found that weight loss *was* actually a significant part of what it was about. No wonder the pounds piled on when I stopped: my joy has always been that if you make sure you run enough each week, you can eat fairly gluttonously and get away with it. Well, surprise, surprise, although my motivation to run vanished, my enthusiasm to eat loads of food stuck about.

More changes came, none of them agreeable. I would become breathless running for a train, and every day I felt the absence of the runners' high. What took me by surprise was how sore and tired my legs felt all the time. Through 15 years of running, including weeks in which my mileage was into the 30s, I had never woken with such heavy legs as I did when I stopped running.

Sometimes, I'd make it out for an embarrassingly breathless 5km (3 miles) on a Monday morning. This would be the week I would bounce back, I'd tell myself. But somehow, for the rest of the week, my running shoes would not move from where I'd left them on the Monday, when I'd arrived home, an unprecedented tsunami of sweat pouring from my bewildered frame.

I really wanted to run, so I could stop feeling portly, morose and wheezy. The only thing was, I felt too portly, morose and wheezy to run. Every time a jogger trotted past me on the street, I felt more defeated and more ashamed. Whenever I saw a Facebook update from a friend about another successful long run, I winced.

After weeks of inertia I tried again, but always setting out in the afternoon. Within a week of this my enthusiasm had returned. At that stage, I moved back to morning running, which suits me best, but that brief move into afternoon running had got me back on track.

Run in the home

AS WE ALL KNOW, running is the most straightforward and accessible form of exercise. You don't need a gym, or teammates or expensive equipment. All you need is some basic kit and you can get out there and run. What's stopping you?

Well actually, the answer is that a lot of things can stop you. Injuries, bad weather or pandemics are just some of the things that make running on the streets a bad idea at times. And even the most committed runner won't necessarily want to get out there every day of their lives.

But this doesn't mean you have to go to pot. Life isn't a binary choice between running 48km (30 miles) each week or lazing on the sofa, filling your face with junk food. Even when you cannot run, or don't want to run, you can still be improving yourself physically and mentally, so that the moment it's fine for you to be out running again, you're ready for it, rather than having to start again.

Here are some tips for the downtimes...

Running on the spot

If you can't – or don't want to – leave the house, that doesn't mean you can't run. You can even run in your living room. Running on the spot is a great way to get your heart rate up and it will also really benefit your leg muscles.

You should approach it in a similar way to usual running. Warm up slowly, by starting at a gentler pace. You might like to throw in some pre- or post-run stretching, too. Once you are up and running (on the spot) you can also replicate interval running by alternating between faster sprints for, say, one minute, followed by two minutes at a gentler pace.

Bear in mind that because running on the spot doesn't require you to use the muscles that propel you to move forwards, you'll be landing on your toes more than you would with normal running. Therefore, running on the spot can help increase ankle and lower leg strength. However, if you run on the spot for too long you can end up with pain in your hips, shins and ankles. So it's probably best to see this as an alternative for days when you cannot or don't want to run outdoors, rather than a lifelong pursuit.

Study running

Even as you lie back on your sofa, you can be making yourself a better runner. You could read a running magazine or listen to a running podcast. Or you could open a discussion in a running group on Facebook, getting answers from other runners to your most burning questions. Or you could even read one of those running book things. I hear some of them are quite good.

Running isn't all about the body, the mind plays a big part, too. So exercising your mind with running information

▷

can be nearly as beneficial as exercising your body with miles on the road.

𝓝on running

According to a study published in the *International Journal of Sports Science*, bouncing is twice as effective at improving aerobic fitness as running. This means that investing in a small trampoline for your home, or a slightly larger one for your garden, can be a good move for a runner.

Bouncing on trampolines is softer on your joints than running, so it gives them a rest while you get a good workout. Plus, they're fun. It's impossible to feel miserable as you bounce on a trampoline. Embrace your inner child and keep bouncing!

Don't do things you're not running far enough for

There are so many running techniques and gimmicks around running nowadays that when you start getting excited about the hobby it's easy to do all sorts of things that are actually quite unnecessary. Or to start buying gadgets and other items that are for runners far more advanced than you are.

Are you a too-early adopter? Here are some of the things to watch out for.

Ice baths

Stepping into an ice bath is hell but after very long distances and gruelling courses, it can help aid recovery. A study published in the journal *Medicine & Science in Sports & Exercise* found they can reduce soreness and repair small tears (microtrauma) in your muscle fibres. However, if you are having an ice bath after a 5km (3-mile) run then you've kind of missed the point. That would be like having chemo for a cold.

Breathing gadgets

There are devices that promise to make you a better runner by creating a resistance when you breathe in. Effectively, they give your breathing muscles a workout by making them work harder – like dumbbells but for your diaphragm. But unless you have an objective problem with breathing and have been advised by an independent expert to try these gadgets, it's probably best to leave them alone.

Running gels

If you are running anything less than 16km (10 miles) then there is little point in using a running gel. These are only supposed to be used to replenish your reserves of glycogen, which you won't have used up in shorter runs. You'll just be wasting money and pumping your body full of stuff that it will probably find hard to process.

Carrying water unnecessarily

There's simply no need to take water with you on a 2km (1.25-mile) jog. Have a drink before you leave and another when you get home. Carrying around a water bottle on such brief ventures is unnecessary and, frankly, weird.

Training masks

These are nothing to do with pandemics. The training mask is designed to increase the intensity of your run by mimicking high-altitude conditions with less oxygen. This can encourage your body to produce more red blood cells, which results in greater muscle efficiency for faster results. All of which is great but if you're just looking for a nice, friendly jog around your local park, this would be a bit OTT.

Don't look for quick fixes

Running is a marathon, not a sprint. (Unless it's a sprint. If it's a sprint, then it's probably a sprint.) But running is not an area of life in which you can find quick fixes that drastically change your performance overnight. Particularly with long-distance running, it is better to fall in love with the long-haul nature of the entire process, rather than hoping that you can improve in a flick of a finger.

For many runners, this is one of running's most attractive qualities: its authenticity and reciprocity. What you put into running you get out of running. If the furthest you can comfortably run is 8km (5 miles), you cannot turn into a marathon runner overnight. There is no quick fix. You have to work at it but as long as you do work at it, you will get there, and when you do finally run that marathon, it will be all the sweeter for the fact that you had to work so long and hard for it.

Don't always focus on the clock

Setting speed targets for yourself can be a great way of motivating yourself. It can also make your running experience more exciting and satisfying. The process of creating a challenge for yourself and then seeing it through is a great way to make running work well for you. Also, some runners find that the mathematics of it is a welcome distraction as they pant their way to glory.

However, just as this way of doing it can bring you satisfaction, it can also bring you disappointment. Even the most accomplished of runners cannot keep up with the clock every time. So if you set yourself time goals, you will probably have days when you punch the air with joy but I can guarantee that there will also be days when you are disappointed.

So if you do go down this road, it is important to make sure you are the boss, rather than the clock. The old saying that 'a watched pot never boils' applies to running as well. If you pay attention to the distance you're running, those miles will never seem to pass, but the moment you stop obsessing about it, the miles just seem to fly by.

In 2005, I ran the Dublin Marathon without a running watch. I also paid no attention to any timer clocks along the route. It was my first marathon and I was just happy to savour the atmosphere and try to finish the distance. I had a wonderful day, it was one of the best of my life. I was pleasantly surprised at the finishing line when I realised I'd done the run in 4 hours 4 minutes.

When I returned in 2006, I was determined to run a sub-4-hour marathon. All I had to do was shave four minutes off my time and I would manage it. How hard could that be? Well, very hard, it turned out. I had my running watch with me and I kept consulting it to check if I was keeping up with the pace required to manage a sub-4-hour finish.

I got more and more frustrated whenever I looked at the watch. By the time I was at the 16km (10-mile) point I was both behind my time target and also as tired as I'd have expected to be at the 32km (20-mile) point. I eventually snarled my way across the finishing line in 4 hours 25 minutes.

So don't be the 2006 Chas, the 2005 Chas was way happier. Make sure you are the boss, not the clock.

Paul Tonkinson

A thing I love about running: The one thing I always return to when it comes to running is what it does to time. I always feel that time spent running occupies a different sphere to normal time. It can fracture and split, you lose track of it. A 45-minute run takes 45 minutes, yet within that 45 minutes time can open up, you can be transported to a realm of such deep kinetic bliss that it will carry you through the day. There are moments in the middle of a long run when it feels like you've been running forever, yet it's only been 10 minutes. The converse to this is that, during an interval session ... 60 seconds can last a lifetime. The 'unforgiving minute', someone wrote a poem about it. There's a magic to every moment spent running. I see it as time nicked from everyday life and added on as a bonus at the end.

A thing I hate about running: Hate is too strong a word but I'm not particularly enjoying running as I get older; the getting slower bit. I'm grateful to run and I always will be but the negotiation with age is proving troublesome. My body's rebelling a bit. It takes way longer to warm up now, the smooth gliding sensation is more fleeting. At times it feels like I'm a parody of my former self. Sometimes I'll spot myself in a shop window as I run past and it's quite a confrontational moment. I'll never get faster. There. That's a tough sentence to write. I don't hate it but it's a struggle.

Paul Tonkinson is a comedian, a co-host of the podcast Running Commentary *and the author of* 26.2 Miles to Happiness: A Comedian's Tale of Running, Red Wine and Redemption.

HOW TO RUN WITH A DOG

One of the joys of my running life has been lining up at the start of parkruns alongside dogs. To exercise alongside a different species feels like such an honour. Not everyone is a fan of dogs at running events but for me, the more animals the better. I only wish I could run alongside other creatures. Imagine galloping with a gazelle or sprinting alongside a donkey. I wouldn't mind trying a 3km (1.8-mile) run with a calf. Ah, one day.

For those of us who grew up watching the *Rocky* movies and for whom Sylvester Stallone's titular hero was an early inspiration, running with a dog seems a marvellous idea because that boxing character would run with Butkus, his Bullmastiff. Man, they looked great together.

However, with so many runners not keen on the presence of dogs at running events, and with your dog's safety being just as important, it is worth following some simple guidelines to make it all run smoothly.

The ages of dog

Wait until your dog is one year old before taking it on a proper run. Before then, its skeleton will not be fully grown. Equally, as your dog approaches the latter years of its life, it's probably time for it to hang up its metaphorical running shoes.

Consider the breed

Some breeds, such as Huskies, gun dogs, Golden Retrievers, Collies and Dalmatians, are natural runners. Some other breeds, particularly Bulldogs and Pugs, are far less suitable for running due to their tendency to have breathing problems. Some breeds also have particular vulnerability to hip problems. So do your research before trying to turn your dog into an athlete.

If in doubt – ask a vet

Vets should be able to tell you whether your dog is suitable as a running companion.

Start gradually

Just like you wouldn't enter a local half marathon if you had never run before, neither should your dog be thrown into the fray too suddenly. Start with gentle walk/jog combinations in quiet, relaxed settings. The fewer the distractions, the more the dog will focus on your commands. Obedience is key for a run with your dog. If your pet is a bit on the rebellious side then joint runs with them might not be the best idea.

Check the conditions

Your dog won't thank you for taking it on a run on a boiling hot day, what with its coat and lack of sweat glands. It's unlikely to be keen on a run on a freezing or icy day, either, and freezing pavements and grit can rip their paw pads. (Always wash your dog's paws if it has walked on grit, as it can be poisonous if they lick their paws afterwards.) Bascially, keep your dog dashes for mild days.

Paws for thought

Dogs' paws are sensitive things. Soil, meadows or sand work well for dog runs. Hot cement in the summer? Not so much.

Aim for cushioned surfaces, and check their pads for cuts, thorns and any signs of damage.

Refresh judiciously

Plenty of water for your dog during and after a run is clearly essential. However, with food it is different. Experts say that as long as you feed your dog a healthy diet and you are not taking it on excessively long runs, there is no need to give them extra food due to the exertions. Also, you shouldn't be taking them on excessively long runs anyway.

Be kind

If your dog shows any sign of exhaustion or discomfort during a run, just call a halt to it. This isn't the time for a motivational talk from a coach. You shouldn't be going all bossy and asking your dog: 'What's wrong with you, come on! Are you a man or a mouse?'

Be aware

It's easy for your dog to trip up another runner or to force other runners off the course. This is bound to cause annoyance. Your dog may rule your household but other people are going to expect him or her to respect them. So avoid getting in the path of other runners.

Take bags

When dogs run, their bladders and bowels are often loosened. Make sure you take bags, in case they suddenly stop and leave a present on the course. This will be embarrassing enough as it is – don't make it worse by not having anything to clean it up with.

The leash you can do

This seems an obvious one but make sure you keep your dog on a leash. If you are taking them to a parkrun or similar event then make sure that leash is tight. It can be hard for dog owners to understand but some people really don't like our lovely pets...

What if ...
a dog runs towards you?

They might be known as man's best friend but dogs are not every runner's friend, best or otherwise. When you're out running and a dog bounds up to you, it's easy to be scared. Even if the dog is small, they can make your ankles and shins suddenly feel very exposed.

Sometimes things can get very serious: runners have been killed by dogs, including a jogger who was mauled to death by two large dogs in Detroit in 2014. As onlookers tried to save him, he told them: 'I'm dying.'

That said, of course, most dogs are harmless. Even if they run towards you they will often get distracted. But to keep safe, here are some tips for how to avoid trouble:

1. Make sure you use a deep, assured tone of voice to communicate calmness and authority. You might feel like screaming but that will agitate the dog more and could trigger their instinct to fight.
2. Other behaviours that could make the dog aggressive include eye contact or, of course, lashing out at them.
3. If your running route and routine are both fairly regular then the chances of you encountering unfamiliar dogs is reduced.

4   Don't engage with the dog more than you have to. Many
    dogs will simply lose interest in anyone who shows no
    interest in them.
5   Once you're ready to move away, do it slowly. Avoid
    sudden movements or turning your back on the dog.
6   Often, because you've been running so fast and are so
    tuned into your run, you can be caught unawares. Stay
    alert to dogs on the run.
7   If a dog does try to attack you, curl into a ball and
    protect your face, chest and throat. Keep your hands in
    fists to protect your fingers. The safest place to be bitten
    is the shin or forearm. A dog bite to the thigh can cause
    fatal bleeding.

Here are some signs that a dog is feeling aggressive:

- Loud barks or growling.
- Increase in body size and erect body posture.
- Displacement behaviour, such as licking its lips or
  yawning.
- Snarling (including bared teeth).
- Head, neck and ears are elevated.
- Stiff, raised tail.

HOW TO RUN INTO OLD AGE

Running in your advancing years can be a joy and a true health
benefit. However, the older you get, the more important it is
to do everything right. Here are some reminders to keep you
fighting fit.

Concentrate on your gait

With balance becoming more important as you get older, senior runners must pay more attention to their running form. As you lose strength in your core, you will become less naturally balanced. Luckily, the mind can make up for that by focusing on a balanced, safe gait.

Check with your GP

There is never any harm in checking with your GP whether you are healthy enough to continue, or start, running.

Consistency is key

A study has found that seniors who are consistent with their running are less likely to develop heart problems. So find a regime that works for you and stick to it as best you can.

Adjust your targets

The distances and paces that you were comfortable with during your 50s won't be so sensible during your 60s and 70s. There is no point pushing yourself too hard to reach goals that are unattainable at your age.

Find softer surfaces

Your legs will thank you if you do as much of your running as possible on softer surfaces, such as tracks, grass and trails. Even the odd run on the dreaded treadmill will be beneficial.

Follow all the basic tips religiously

When you are a younger runner you might be able to get away with not stretching or hydrating properly, or with not taking rest days. But as you get into your 60s and beyond, you have to stick to all the basic running advice.

Focus on recovery

Of all the basic tips that you should pay special attention to as you get older, recovery is the biggest.

Build strength

As you grow older, you lose muscle mass. OK, so you might not be planning to flex your muscles on the beach during your next holiday, but a lack of muscle mass is not good news if you want to carry on running. For instance, weak calves and ankles will increase your risk of injury. Basic leg strengthening exercises and gentle weight training will help keep you muscled up.

Get a running partner

Safety becomes more important for older runners. If there are two of you, you can support one another and also keep each other safe.

GUEST FEATURE *Henry Winter*

A thing I love about running: I love the unexpected. Whenever I visit a city to cover a football match, I check into the hotel and get my running shoes on. You see life out running, see things, experience all things. I've been chased by dogs in Tbilisi. I've been kicked by a monk in Kobe. I've run laps of the roof of the Fiat factory in Turin used for the Minis scene in *The Italian Job*. I've run through districts of Moscow, Saint Petersburg and Volgograd where locals stare suspiciously at a tourist walking, but a knackered-looking runner? Carry on, mad man.

A thing I hate about running: The knowledge that my knees will soon creak their last, that I will have to stop running and I won't get to do another New York or London Marathon or another Great North Run. I won't experience the buzz of those atmospheres again, the head-clearing joy and ability to see a city from another angle. Cycling and swimming will not stop me mourning the end of my running days.

Henry Winter is the chief football writer of The Times.

HEALTH AND SAFETY

In a previous section, the *Code* showed you how to take care of others as you run. Now, we turn to how to take care of yourself. Yep, it's time to turn our attention back to little old you.

Find out how to run with a cold without making it worse and how to run safely in the dark, the wet and the burning sun. Discover how to avoid injury and what to do if you have overtrained.

Learn how caffeine can be used as mid-run pain relief, why Vitamin D is important and why it's safe to drink and run. It's important to keep safe, so here is your *Code* for doing so. It's time for those words that everyone dreams of hearing: here is your Health and Safety briefing.

PREVENTION IS BETTER THAN CURE

The second-best time to take injury seriously is just after you've picked one up. The best time is right now. No runner wants to be taken out of action so here's how to be a happy and healthy runner all year round.

10 ways to avoid injury

Sometimes you will get injured because of sheer bad luck but often it will be because you did something wrong. Here are some basic ways to avoid being that runner who glares enviously at other runners when you're crocked.

1. Make sure you warm up and cool down.
2. Drink plenty of water – because when you are properly hydrated you'll be less likely to get cramp, which can lead to further injury problems.
3. Don't run on crowned roads, where the pavement slopes from the middle to the left and right. The surface is more uneven than you might realise mid-run and it can cause issues with your gait that translate into injuries.
4. Stay alert as you run. Many injuries come about because of poor running gait. Check your posture and check you're not slouching.
5. Don't wear super-light running shoes. Don't believe the hype that these will shave a few seconds off

your finish time. They're more likely to send you to the physio's treatment table.

6. Always run in running shoes. Any old trainers are not running shoes. Only running shoes are running shoes.

7. Make sure your shoes fit properly. Most injuries come about because of poor foot function, so make sure yours are cased well.

8. Don't do speedwork during every run.

9. Build your leg muscle strength with exercises, including squats and lunges.

10. Take time off. This doesn't just mean rest days during the week – you should also factor in a week off during your annual running calendar.

Look out for obstacles

Scandalously, town planning is not based around the whims of the runner. In fact, there are obstacles galore out there, just waiting to disrupt the natural flow of your run. Here's how to tackle them.

Traffic light crossings

It's a great day when the lights go red just as you approach the crossing, allowing you to cross the road without shifting pace at all. It's also a rare day. If you have to wait you can always run on the spot. You might look like a prat – you *will* look like a prat – but you will keep moving.

Zebra crossings

Deep into a run, it can be easy to lose your sense of safety. Don't just burst across the road, assuming drivers will stop for you. Approach them as carefully as you would at any other time.

Bollards
It's great that you feel all giddy and happy 13km (8 miles) into your run but don't be tempted to frog-jump that bollard. The stakes are way too high.

Hills
Everyone knows it's hard to run up a hill but few know that it's also tricky to run down a hill. We've all seen someone pick up too much momentum on the way down. Take care and watch your footing!

Mud
Yes, it can be fun to run through mud. We are so conditioned to avoid getting dirty that it can feel enormously liberating to set out deliberately to get messy. However, mud can be dangerous – particularly if you don't notice that your foot has just got stuck and you try to continue regardless.

Watch your feet
Whether you run in the park or on pavement, the ground is full of hidden dangers. Concealed tree roots can send you flying, hidden potholes can make you tumble and a change of terrain can make you stumble. So keep some attention on the ground.

Make sleep part of your training
A great thing about running is that running helps you sleep better and sleeping helps you run better. What a virtuous circle. So, whether you want to thrive as a runner, or as a sleeper, you

really should concentrate on performing better in bed. No, I don't mean *that* way.

A study published in the *Journal of Clinical Sleep Medicine* has found that regular exercise can improve the quality of your sleep and help you sleep through the night. In fact, as little as 30 minutes of moderate aerobic exercise may result in a difference in sleep quality that same night. However, it can take up to four months for your body to get used to the increased activity level. So if you are new to running, don't be disheartened if you haven't enjoyed this benefit yet.

Once you've nodded off, exercise can give you more slow-wave sleep – that deep sleep, when the brain and body have a chance to rejuvenate. Exercise can also help to stabilise your mood and decompress the mind.

The science and data is just as encouraging when you come at it from the other way round. A study for the journal *Medicine & Science in Sports & Exercise* found that sleeping for an extra 75 minutes on six consecutive nights can help your performance ahead of a marathon. This is because your muscles grow while you sleep. Also, when you haven't slept properly, you're more likely to eat more: sleep researchers at the New York Obesity Nutrition Research Center found that people who are sleep-deprived consume around 300 calories more per day. That's not going to help you get fit.

Clearly, then, it's important to make sleep part of your training routine. There are many ways to sleep (and therefore run) better. For instance, have a consistent bedtime hour and routine, consider blackout curtains and make sure your bedroom is at a comfortable temperature. Want to avoid those bleary-eyed visits to the toilet during the night? Cut back on liquid consumption three hours before bedtime.

When you get into bed, don't sit scrolling social media on your phone. It will unsettle you emotionally and the light from your phone will make your subsequent sleep less rewarding. Experts suggest that you power off TVs, laptops and tablets an hour before bedtime.

Put a bit of time and attention into what you do between the sheets and the rewards will be obvious. Make sleep part of your running routine.

Bask in the post-run nap
One of the joys of the long run is the rest afterwards. Don't regard this as a naughty indulgence, consider it as part of the process. As we have seen, sleep is part of the recovery process after any vigorous workout. Your muscles rebuild during this time, so you can run again another day.

Make sure you rest
Running regularly is great. Running every day is dangerous. Take regular days off. If you find it hard, just remind yourself that the very best thing you can do for your running on these days is not to run. You are training by not training.

TO RUN OR NOT TO RUN?

When runners wake up with a sore throat or a sniffle, some immediately and gleefully shelve any plans they had to run that day. 'You mean I have an excuse for a lie-in?' they think. 'Well that is marvellous news!' They then put their head back on the pillow and fall back asleep.

Logically, this makes perfect sense. When you have a bug, your body is going to need a lot of energy to fight it, so it needs to conserve all the energy it can to get you back to good health. Diverting energy to head out for a 10km (6-mile) run is not going to help.

But not all runners have perfect sense, do we? There are many runners who are absolutely determined to get out there despite any sickness. For some of us, it can be quite a challenge to stay indoors, even when we're under the weather. Non-runners think that running is torture. For many runners, *not* running is torture.

We miss our fix of runners' high. We get bored lying in bed all day. We fear that if we stop running for too long we will lose the levels of fitness and reserves of stamina we have spent so long building up. We become haunted by images of us being humbled back to a beginner's level: getting out of breath after a a few minutes of running. And let's be honest, we worry about getting fat.

This runners' paranoia can drag many a stricken runner out of their sick bed and out on to the streets. Well, if you're determined to get out there and if you are quite sure it's just a cold, as opposed to a Covid, there are some simple steps you can take to make it safer.

How to run (or not) with a cold

The standard benchmark for many runners is what is known as the 'neck check': if your cold symptoms are above the neck, it's usually safe to run. However, if your symptoms are below your neck, you shouldn't run.

Running in the first three days of a cold is usually fine. In fact, it can be a good idea because you can open your airways and help get rid of the bug. This is because running helps your body to decongest by allowing the mucus and phlegm to clear out. That's why if you run with a cold, you soon find yourself expelling plenty of goo from your throat and nose. It's not pretty, but it's definitely a healthy way to go. Just make sure you dispose of it with as much dignity and decency as you can manage (i.e. carry tissues).

Also, running and similar forms of cardio exercise release an adrenaline called epinephrine, which is a natural decongestant. So, if you have a blocked nose, runny nose or sore throat then a run should help you clear up the symptoms a bit.

However, if you have a painful chest, aching muscles or a high temperature you shouldn't be going anywhere near your running shoes. Just leave them by the door, rest up and get better. At the most, you should consider a brisk walk. But really, do you need to do anything? There is an annoying martyr-like energy around the runner who insists on getting out there even when they are feeling ill. It's all a bit boarding-school-masochist and definitely one of those times when the exasperated sighs of non-runners are understandable.

So: to run or not to run? The key to making the right call is fearless honesty. It's possible for any of our minds to convince us that we are sicker than we really are but it's also easy for us to tell ourselves that we are less ill than we truly are. Listen to your body and your conscience. You really don't need to have trained as a doctor to be able to make this decision.

Even if you have decided you can safely head out with your symptoms, that doesn't mean you should run at full pace or for a long distance. Just run at a steady, comfortable pace over a short or medium distance.

Also, this is probably not the right time to run with a group or at an event. You don't want to put yourself in any athletic scenario that might tempt you to run beyond your sensible comfort zone. Running with others, particularly during a timed event, can make anyone go at it harder than they should. In any case, it's clearly unkind to turn up to a group run when you are infectious. Dear me, long-distance running events can be absolute horror movies for infection. Remember the scene: hoards of sweaty, panting runners, commending each other with high fives, hugs and even kisses. Meanwhile, well-wishing spectators bawl out encouragement and offer their own physical congratulations. So many lurgies must be passed around, it's a miracle that everyone involved doesn't simply collapse on the spot.

Returning to running

After you have taken time off because of a bug then the advice is similar to that for when you return to running following injury. Start again gently and gradually. Say you were running 24km (15 miles) per week before you got sick. You shouldn't be looking for a mileage anywhere near that high as you start up again. Your pace should also be slower than it was before you were struck down with the sniffles and your runs should be less frequent. This is no time to sprint.

Immunity made simple

But here's the good news – being a moderate runner will probably make you less likely to be struck down by a bug in the first place because it can boost your immune system in the short and long term. This does depend, though, on how long and far you run: while 30–45 minutes of moderate daily exercise positively stimulates the immune system, too much running at longer distances temporarily weakens it. This is because the strain of a hard run causes the body to produce the stress hormone cortisol, which actively suppresses immune function.

The mathematics of it all can be a little dazzling. Just a matter of seconds into your run, your immune cells multiply up to tenfold. However, cynics point out that after you finish your run, those immune cells decrease to below-normal levels, sometimes by as much as 50 per cent, for some hours before levelling off at normal levels. Here's the plot twist: those missing cells haven't disappeared. In fact, they are getting busy: they are engaged in what's called 'immune surveillance' – when they rush about the bloodstream looking for infection.

There are great ways of giving your body an immunity boost straight after a run. Antioxidants are important and there are bars that are crammed full of these helpful goodies, such as selenium, vitamin E and others. Everyday foods rich in antioxidants include nuts, dried fruits and blueberries. However, the fact remains that after a long run you are at risk for a few days afterwards. So, if you've run a marathon, you're most vulnerable to getting sick for up to 72 hours after the event because of your elevated cortisol levels. Just be careful during that period. You don't need to go into full Covid-19-style lockdown, but perhaps avoid any kids' birthday parties and call a three-day moratorium on licking door handles.

Don't panic!

Do you find you cough after finishing a run? This doesn't necessarily mean you're coming down with a cold – or something worse. You are probably suffering from bronchoconstriction: the small muscles lining your lungs get a spasm. This is a natural part of the experience for many runners and doesn't mean you're about to die.

Recognise the symptoms of overtraining

You may already have heard the joke. A physio is asked what the most popular form of training is for runners, and they reply: overtraining. It's surprisingly easy to overdo it. Non-runners sometimes ask runners how we motivate ourselves to get out there and run. However, the truth is that for a lot of us, we are more likely to need to motivate ourselves *not* to run.

Overtraining occurs when a runner exceeds their body's ability to recover from strenuous exercise. It conjures a host of horrors, both physical and emotional. The irony is that you are most in danger of overtraining at the exact time that you can least afford to do it: when you are preparing for a big event. Many a runner has had their worst brush with overtraining in the months leading up to a marathon, when they push themselves too hard.

Overtraining is quite the enemy for the runner. Here is how to recognise it, and what to do about it.

An elevated resting heart rate

If you own a smart watch, it is easier than ever to take your pulse rate. If you have been overtraining, you will begin to notice a slight spike. If you register an increase in your morning pulse rate of 10bpm or more, you've probably overtrained.

Frequent bugs

A nasty consequence of overtraining is a dip in your immune system. So if you suddenly keep picking up colds, flu and other bugs, and if you find them harder than usual to shift, then overtraining may be to blame. (And if ever there were a time in human history to make sure you avoid being prone to infection, this is it.)

Disturbed sleep
Overtraining really messes with your sleep. During the day, you keep wanting to nod off but when you get into bed at night you can't sleep properly. You wake up in the early hours, feeling like your heart is racing. It's a non-stop frustration. Again, a smart watch can help you monitor this problem, so you can reassure yourself it's not your imagination.

Lowered sex drive
Speaking of bedtime, if you are getting less and less interested in rumpy-pumpy between the sheets, then that might be a sign of overtraining, too.

Grumpiness
Do you keep bickering with your partner? Are you currently tied up in dozens of arguments on social media? Are you worried human resources are going to call you in for a 'quick chat'? Have you even fallen out with your goldfish? Looks like you've overtrained, pal.

Poorer perceptions
You feel like you're running harder but your stats are getting worse. No, your sports watch isn't broken, you are. This is why another term for overtraining is unexplained underperformance syndrome (UPS).

Knackered legs

Are your pegs sore and tight? Or do they feel super heavy when you are out running? Are little muscular twinges and niggles taking forever to clear up? Now you know why.

Change in hunger levels

Generally, a lack of hunger is regarded as a clear sign of overtraining but an increase in hunger can also be a dead giveaway. So, if you are feeling significantly less hungry or more hungry than you should, then you've probably pounded too many pavements.

Fuzzy memory

If you find your ... what's the word for it ... memory keeps ... messing up, then ... what was I saying? Mate, you've overtrained.

Rest

This is the most obvious advice: if you are training too hard then the simple answer is to rest for a while. However, for many runners this is much easier said than done. 'Surely a little 5K couldn't hurt,' we think, even as our body screams at us to give it a bit of time off. So put your feet up and relax. Remind yourself that for these days, the very best thing you can do for your running is not run.

Bathe

Long soaks in warm baths will be good for your body, your mind and your soul. So do it. Add some nice pampering bath oil or healthy salts to make it luxurious. Maybe add some candles and relaxing panpipe music, too?

Eat and hydrate well

Your body needs you to restock it with plenty of fluid and healthy grub. Treat it like a temple for a few days. (Albeit a somewhat sickly temple.)

Start again gently

When you do get back out there, don't emerge with a vengeance and start tearing it up again. Avoid hills, long runs and tempo work for a while. Just go out on gentle, short runs and let your body get back into the groove.

In short: overtraining is a great opportunity to hone your ability to listen to your body rather than your mind. Your mind might be telling you to run more and to go harder but your body is screaming that you should do the opposite. The body never lies, so when the mind and body are at odds, always listen to the body.

HOW TO RUN IN THE RAIN

Running in the rain is another of those things that non-runners imagine is so much harder than it is. In fact, they assume that running in anything less than ideal weather conditions is some special form of hell. This really isn't the case. On a warm day, it can be rather refreshing when there is a sudden downpour. Some people actually prefer running in the rain. Public school people, mostly.

Runners are among the world's most avid devotees of weather apps. I have three downloaded on to my phone and have strong opinions about which of them is most accurate at forecasting rain and which is best at predicting temperatures. (Very strong opinions. Never get stuck with me at a party.)

But whether you're a fan or not of the rain, you can't let the weather dictate your running schedule too much. A veteran of 20 Boston marathons was once asked whether he skipped a run if it was raining. 'If you start skipping runs because the weather's too lousy pretty soon you start missing runs because the weather's too nice,' he replied.

It's true. You should not duck out of a run just because it's raining. That said, running in the rain does bring particular dangers, so make sure you follow the *Code*.

Safety first

Visibility for drivers is impaired in the wet, so don't assume they can see you. It takes cars longer to brake on wet roads, so keep that in mind, too. Besides, drivers are less likely to expect people to be out and about during very wet weather.

Protect your valuables

Be careful with your gadgets during a downpour. It's fine to get your phone out to quickly change the music from one act to another, but don't take too long over it. Get it tucked away from the rain as soon as possible.

Lube your feet

Some runners apply petroleum jelly to their feet before a run in particularly rainy conditions, to prevent blisters or chafing.

| *Claire Maxted*

A thing I love about running: I love exploring new landscapes through running – there is nothing more exciting than doing a race in a new place, or getting the map out, planning a new route and seeing new countryside or mountain views for the first time. What really appeals to me is a good mix of different types of trails and terrain. I love skinny, twisting woodland paths, tracks alongside rivers or lakes, a bit of fun scrambling up a mountain or hillside, and then an excitingly rocky descent that you have to really focus on not to go flying. That and a nice bit of cake and a pint afterwards – the perfect run!

A thing I hate about running: Blisters on multi-day ultras has been a biggie for me. How can something so small cause so much agony? Blisters have made my running so, so miserable that I have quit two multi-day ultras now. My little toes for some reason tuck slightly under my other toes, and when my feet swell up by day four, I get a ginormous, painful blister on each side, which I tread on with each footstep. It's like stepping on knives while being stung in the foot by a trapped wasp. I really need to get a bigger pair of shoes, use toe-socks and protect my little toes with K-tape, but part of me doesn't even dare do another multi-day ultra to test this solution!

Claire Maxted is the author of The Ultimate Trail Running Handbook *and director of* Wild Ginger Running *trail and ultra running YouTube channel.*

Match your expectations to the weather

If you were planning to run at a new PB pace but it's pouring with rain or there's a howling gale then it might be worth postponing that target for a drier day. Rain and the wind won't help.

Get in the bin

If it's rainy on the day of your event, take along a bin liner with holes punched in it for your head and arms. You can stay dry under that during that lull between you lining up at the start and actually getting going. If you've stayed in a hotel the night before the marathon, nab the shower cap for the same purpose. You can (considerately) dispose of both just before countdown and you won't look *that* stupid.

Stuff your shoes

When you have returned home, remove the soles of your running shoes and stuff the shoes full of newspaper, to help them dry out quickly.

What if ...
lightning strikes?

We hear a lot about how unlikely it is that you'd be struck by lightning. David Hand's book *The Improbability Principle* suggested the odds are 300,000/1 but the *British Medical Journal* suggests that it is actually far less likely: a 10,000,000/1 shot.

However unlikely it is to happen, though, lightning can kill you if it strikes. So if you are out running and a major thunderstorm stirs up, here are some simple steps to keep yourself safer:

- Go home.
- Avoid open spaces.
- Don't shelter under a tall, isolated tree.
- Don't hide in a metal shed.
- Head to a substantial building or car.

HOW TO RUN IN THE DARK

Some people can only fit in a run in the evening. Others just plain prefer to run after dark. This is fine, but there are specific safety guidelines you should follow before you set off for a night-time dash.

Leave your AirPods at home

You need to be able to hear if cars, animals or weirdos are around you. If you are busy listening to music or chatter, you're making it too difficult. Even if you are a dedicated listener to music or podcasts as you run, this is not the time to do it. However much you think you can stay alert, you will be distracted if you are plugged in. If you feel you absolutely have to have some audio distraction, keep the volume as low as you can.

Make yourself visible

It's more important than ever for drivers and other pedestrians to see you, so make sure you wear brightly coloured hi-visibility clothing when you run in the dark. Ideally, your night-time running gear will have reflective detailing, too. Make sure you're visible from the front and the back so both directions of traffic will see you.

Some runners also invest in a head torch, which has the dual benefit of making you more visible while lighting up the path ahead of you. This reduces the chance of tripping over an obstacle.

Run with others

Whether it's with a running club or just an informal group of friends, you'll find that when it comes to running at night, there really is safety in numbers.

Take your phone

Even if you generally like the freedom of being uncontactable as you run, a night-time run is not the time for this. You will never regret having a phone on a run in the dark but there's a chance you will regret not having one. It's easy to take phones on runs now. Do it.

Tell someone where you're going

It's always a good idea to tell someone where you're going. Whether it's a quick text to a friend or letting someone at home know, ask them to contact you if they don't hear from you if you are late in returning.

Choose a well-lit route

This one seems like a no-brainer. During the day, you are free to choose from a number of routes for your run but in the dark, you should only choose a well-lit one. Those semi-concealed tree roots in your local park will have you flat on your face if you can't see them. Also, you're less likely to be mugged or come into contact with dodgy people in illuminated areas.

Trust your instincts
If something doesn't feel right, get the hell out of the area.

Leave jewellery and other valuables at home
In the unlikely event that you are robbed you'll be comforted not to have lost your favourite keepsakes.

Run with a dog
If you are going to run with a dog then the darker hours could be a good time to do it. A would-be aggressor will think twice about approaching you if you've got a big beast at your side. Also, there will be fewer innocent people around to get scared by your dog.

Carry ID
The chances of an emergency are slim but if you have contact information and details of any allergies or health conditions, it will help. If you are away from home on holiday or business, make a note of the hotel in which you are staying.

GUEST FEATURE *Jonathan Cairns*

A thing I love about running: Well in my first year I could have answered that in one word: nothing. So why did you run, you might ask? Because I had set myself a goal of running 5km (3 miles) without stopping.

Because I was failing left, right and centre in my life and I desperately had to attempt something that was so far out of my skill set that I couldn't see how I was going to accomplish it. Then I needed to accomplish it, for me.

But things have changed since then. The act of getting out and running regularly in those early days became a part of me. Running is now something that I do, because it is me. I'm also the sort of person who likes to have something to look forward to. Trips, holidays, races, nights out, weekend runs with friends etc.

I spend my days working in a hospital and I don't always like the atmosphere there. Every day when the going gets rough I look at my watch and think, in a few more hours I will be out running. My skin will be tingling with the cold air, my lungs will be loving the oxygen and I will cherish every breath without a mask. There is nothing like a hospital to give you an appreciation of good health.

So to hone in on one thing that I love about running it's this – it's not a place or a thing, it's an act. The act of running is something no one can do for you. You feel it, suffer it, celebrate it, inhale it and exhale it, every single step.

A thing I hate about running: One night I got home from work and it was dark and bitterly cold. There was a storm warning and in the frenzied wind the rain was coming down, across and even up. I changed and went out, bringing a head torch with me. I was tired and had little energy and found it difficult to run with such an angry wind. I headed down to the river Dodder and into Bushy Park where I thought I might get some shelter. The darkness was complete and only my head torch kept me on the path. The river raged beside me and although I could barely see it, the energy and sound didn't let me forget that it was not to be messed with.

There is a section of stepping stones where it's possible to cross the river. When I got there, in the middle of the 10 stones, there was a large branch of a tree stuck between two stones. As the light from my torch reached it, to my horror I saw a rat sitting on the branch. It jumped into the raging water and swam towards the light. I watched for a few seconds, frozen in fear. 'Oh my God,' I thought, 'it's swimming just under the surface and heading for me.'

I am terrified of rats and up to that point I thought they would stay away from people given the choice. I turned and ran, fast. Every 100m (109 yards) or so I stopped and turned to see if the rat was chasing me. I couldn't hear anything because the blowing trees and the river were deafening. I knew somewhere that I was being ridiculous but I couldn't help it. I didn't relax until I got home with my front door shut.

In my first book, *The Plant-based Runner*, I wrote about the discipline that it takes for me to achieve my goals. It is a constant battle and I go to war every day with my desire to relax on the couch. Regardless of the weather or how I feel, I go out as planned. I believe that if I let those commitments to myself slip, before I know it, the foundations would be gone and I could be free falling in other parts of my life. I hate the way running points out this fault in my personality and prevents me from putting off my planned run by even one day.

Jonathan Cairns is the author of **The Plant-based Runner.**
www.jcruns.com

HOW TO RUN IN THE COLD

Running when the temperature drops can be truly exhilarating and has the added benefit of the fact that there will be fewer pedestrians out and about getting in your way, fewer insects to fly up your nose, and you won't overheat as easily. That said, there are sometimes additional hazards and considerations you need to assess before you set out.

PS – The flipside of this advice is that just as you must not run during wintry days when the surfaces are dangerous, you really *must* run on the days when all is safe. During the winter months you can never be sure how safe it will be in the days and weeks ahead, so when there is a dry, bright day, with no ice at all, make sure you get out there and do some miles.

Still rehydrate on cool days

When you are out running on a hot, dry day, you don't need to be reminded to keep hydrating. You only need to run a few miles in those conditions before your body is crying out for some nice, cool water. However, on colder days, it's easy to forget, but you still need to drink plenty of water.

HOW TO RUN IN THE SUN

As you throw the curtains open, a ray of gorgeous sunlight beams into your room. It's a beautiful day out there and all you can think of is getting out and running in the sun. And why wouldn't you want to? The temperature will be pleasant, the scenery will be extra beautiful and everyone will be in a great mood. However, there are a few downsides, so here's how to stay safe while soaking up those rays.

The bright side of the sun

Vitamin D is vital for health and a run in the sun is a great – and free – way of loading up on it. A lack of vitamin D can lead to depression, bone fractures, hypertension, autoimmune diseases and cancer. It was also connected to worse cases of Covid-19. Running in the sun can also help reduce blood pressure and lower the risk of heart attack and stroke.

The dark side of the sun

That aside, however, there is no doubt that too much sun exposure is dangerous. Yes, you will be able to get a tan but you'll also be able to get skin cancer – especially if, like many runners, you spend more time than usual exposed to the sun. This is backed up by the science. A study in *Archives of Dermatology* found that long-distance runners showed increased numbers of abnormal moles and age spots, putting them at higher risk for malignant melanoma.

Exposure to the sun isn't the only factor here. Long-term running can suppress the immune system, increasing vulnerability to skin damage. What's more, ultraviolet rays can also contribute to cataracts and other eye damage, according to research published in *Clinical, Cosmetic and Investigational Dermatology*.

Slap on some sunscreen

It sounds obvious, but you'd be amazed how few runners do actually wear specially formulated high-factor sports sunscreen. Go for one that won't wash off when you sweat, and make sure you apply it well in advance, before you set out. You should also be wearing it during cooler sunny months, as the damage caused by the sun's rays can still be high even when the mercury is fairly low.

Don your cap

If you are running on a very sunny day then in addition to trying to choose a shady route, such as in a forest, it's a good plan to wear a running cap to protect your face. It will also soak up some of the sweat and stop it streaming into your eyes, and may provide enough eye shade for you to be able to ditch the sunglasses – which may be good news as these can steam up.

Some runners complain that their head can sometimes get overheated when wearing a cap, but that's no excuse. Either buy one with a mesh top to allow circulation, or else just take it off while you're in deep shade and then pop it back on your head when you emerge back into direct sunlight.

GUEST FEATURE *John Brewer*

A thing I love about running: Running fast. In my younger days, I was a half-decent middle-distance runner, capable of running two laps of the track at sub-4 minute-mile pace, but sadly not able to sustain that pace for the four laps that would probably have gained me an international vest. Some 40 years later, I still like to think that I can run at the same speed, although unfortunately the reality is very different. We live close to a disused

World War Two airfield, which was once used to train Wellington bomber pilots. I love to start at one end of the main runway and accelerate down the flat concrete expanse, gradually increasing my stride rate and length, to a speed that feels fast and relaxed, with the breeze blowing through the hair that I no longer have. I like to imagine that anyone watching thinks they are seeing an Olympic athlete doing a speed session; the reality is just an old bald chap out for a fast jog. I then have a few fabulous minutes of what feels to me like fast, flowing and relaxed running, until I reach a point about halfway down the runway where the Wellington's were defying gravity and reaching for the skies, at which point I succumb to fatigue, oxygen deprivation and lactic acid. My stride length soon shortens and my brief experience of speed soon comes to an end. Still, it was great fun while it lasted!

A thing I hate about running: Running in the heat. I once ran a race during which I succumbed to 'hyperthermia' – a condition whereby the body's temperature rises to a dangerously high level. This temperature increase occurs when heat that the body produces when it generates the energy that is needed for running cannot be lost quickly enough. It could be the memory of this unfortunate incident, or a physiological trait that simply prevents me from losing heat quickly and easily, but either way I always do my best to avoid running anything other than short distances when the weather is hot, or worse still, hot and humid.

John Brewer is the author of Run Smart: Using Science to Improve Performance and Expose Marathon Running's Greatest Myths.

LEARN TO IDENTIFY COMMON INJURIES

Some people manage to go through decades of running without developing any injuries. Others can barely get a mile down the road before picking up another knock. For the latter group, running is less about powering along the pavement and more about rubbing ice along their muscles and necking another anti-inflammatory.

Whichever camp you fall into, the *Code* believes that every runner should have a basic understanding of common running injuries. The following is intended to get you started.

Runner's knee (patellofemoral syndrome)

Pain in one or both knees that can range from dull and mild to intense and nasty could mean you've got runner's knee. You will often notice it particularly after a run or after a long period of sitting. Non-runners are so obsessed with running being bad for your knees that lots of out-of-shape people will give you told-you-so looks if you mention you've a knee problem. (For more on this, *see* p. 187.)

Achilles tendinitis

This injury, which often rears its ugly head when you suddenly increase the distance or intensity of your runs, involves inflammation of the tendon that connects your calf muscle to your heel.

If you have pain in your lower leg above the heel, or a feeling of swelling or heat in that area, then you might have Achilles tendinitis. Get it seen to, because if you ignore this one you could end up needing surgery.

Shin splints

Got pain along the front or the inner parts of your lower legs, along your shin bone? Sounds like you've got shin splints.

Other characteristics of shin splints are that the pain gets worse when you exercise, making the shin bone area swollen and tender to the touch. If you get this one, console yourself with the knowledge that it is also a common injury among rock stars, because of all that jumping they do. And get yourself to a doctor, and rest.

Hamstring strains

If as you run you repeatedly cause small tears in the fibres and connective tissue of the hamstring muscle, you will eventually end up with a hamstring strain. Watch out for pain and tenderness in the back of your upper leg.

Plantar fasciitis

It may sound like a form of Nazism that breaks out in a greenhouse but plantar fasciitis is actually a very common form of foot injury.

The thick layer of tissue, called fascia, on the bottom of your foot acts as a spring as you run. If that tissue gets harmed by you running too hard, you can end up with pain under your heel or midfoot, including a burning sensation on the bottom of your foot. Often, the pain will be worst in the morning.

IT band syndrome

No, this isn't the tendency of IT geeks to form disappointing rock bands. Although that is a trend that should be taken seriously, it rather falls outside the remit of the *Code*. IT band syndrome is what happens when the long piece of connective tissue that runs from your outer hip to your knee gets injured and gives you a sharp pain just above your knee. That pain typically gets worse when you bend your knee.

Stress fractures

These sound serious, and they are. They are hairline cracks that form in your bone, typically at the top of the foot, or in the heel or lower leg, due to repetitive stress or impact. If you have worsening pain, swelling, bruising or tenderness in any of those areas then get yourself an X-ray.

SIMPLE INJURY-PREVENTION METHODS

Most ways of avoiding getting hurt are neither complicated nor costly. If you warm up, run on sensible surfaces and avoid taking on too many miles at once, you can keep yourself in the park and away from the physiotherapist's table.

Warm up before you run

If you were going to be given bad news, you'd like to be prepared, right? Do the same favour for your body before you set off on a run.

Choose soft surfaces

Opt for a running route that includes gentler surfaces, such as grass or gravel. Your knees will thank you for it.

Cross-train

Including a non-running form of exercise in your weekly schedule will improve your aerobic fitness, give your joints a break and bestow you with a more balanced physique. So swim, cycle or get on the crosstrainer.

GUEST FEATURE | *Sean Conway*

A thing I love about running: It's 6 a.m. I've been up since 4.30 a.m. with a toddler who decided he wanted to have a rave. Now at 6 a.m. he's decided that maybe 4.30 a.m. was a bit early to get up and he's now back in la-la land. I, however, am now up. I head to the kitchen and open the curtains. Rain slams against the window. It seems we're in the middle of storm Ellen. Mmmmm? The plan was to go for a bike ride today. That seems like a silly idea. Perhaps I'll go for a run. Ten minutes later I'm out the door and heading up the Clwydian Range. Damn it, the weather is crap. It's cold, miserable and my face feels like I've lost a slap-off with Mike Tyson. And you know what? I bloody love it. It's the best thing about running, you can do it in any conditions and I find the worse the weather, the better I feel about it.

> *A thing I hate about running:* It's 3.58 a.m. and
> I'm up and on my bike again for the 24th day in a row,
> cycling 6000km (3730 miles) across Europe. I cycle all
> day before eventually falling asleep in a drainpipe on the
> side of the road that I'm certain is also a wolf lair. I love
> that about cycling. You can go all day. I get back from my
> Europe ride and decide I need to get back on the fells but
> my knees say no. I can't even manage four hours before
> having to stop. This is new to me. I'm used to cycling
> 18 hours a day. It annoys me that I can't go until I literally
> fall asleep. The injury gods seem to have put a hold on my
> running ambition for now. That annoys me about running.
>
> *Sean Conway is an endurance adventurer, motivational speaker
> and the author of several books, including* Running Britain.

Increase mileage slowly

Never increase your weekly mileage by more than 10 per cent
in one go.

Don't ignore possible injuries

Got a nagging pain somewhere in your body? Don't go into
denial and hope it just disappears of its own accord. Sometimes
these niggles do just that but often they develop into something
much more serious.

Work on your gait

Some people have a naturally graceful running technique. Others
have peculiar gaits. You can find out which you are by hiring a
running coach or getting a friend to film you on their phone.

Don't overdo hydration

Clearly, drinking enough water is important for the runner. On both running days and non-running days alike, being hydrated and refreshed is very important. However, you can drink too much water and the result can be lethal: your blood's salt levels can drop to dangerously low levels and bring on a condition called hyponatraemia. Although this is rare, it does hit some athletes, with smaller runners and those who combine running and walking in hot weather particularly prone to it.

Also, if you drink too much water then you are going to keep needing to stop during your run for a public pee. This is awkward for you and potentially distressing for any unwitting eye witnesses.

So, here's the *Code*: Drink water. Drink plenty of water. But don't drink too much water.

When and how to pop pills

FROM ENERGY-BOOSTERS to painkillers, there are many tablets that can help you along the way in your running life without sending you down the path of the pill-popping cheat. Here's what to take and what not to take.

Use caffeine as in-run pain relief

Long runs can often equal pain but when you're 26km (16 miles) into a 32km (20-mile) race, the last thing you want to do is give in and stop.

Some people carry painkillers with them on long runs, to get them through any miles after the pain kicks in, but this is far from ideal health-wise, plus the medication is also

▶

more likely to make you feel drowsy or tired, which is far from ideal running-wise.

Fortunately, there is a way of killing all of these birds with one stone. A study in the *International Journal of Sport Nutrition and Exercise Metabolism* found that caffeine reduces exercise-related pain during workouts. This is because caffeine actually blocks the brain's receptors for adenosine, which is the chemical released by inflammation. So, for long runs, take caffeine pills and water to neck them with, or simply swallow some caffeine sports gels.

Don't overdose on anti-inflammatories

The dosage isn't a suggestion, it's an order. If you take even a little bit too much, you risk heartburn, nausea, vomiting and dizziness. If you take even more than that, you risk convulsions, hypotension and a coma. So don't do it!

What if ...
you get a long-term injury?

Many runners dread getting a long-term injury that rules them out of their favourite pastime for months, years or even for good. Here's how to cope if you are one of the unlucky ones.

Keep in touch with running

Listening to podcasts, volunteering at running events or watching running-related movies can all be great ways to keep connected to running while you wait until you can start to run again yourself.

Walk

So many of the benefits of running still apply to long walks. You get fresh air, you get to see beautiful scenery, you lose weight, your heart gets a workout. So, assuming it's safe to do so, go for some long walks. Take the time you spent running each week and walk for the same amount of time. You'll cover fewer miles but you'll get so many benefits.

Get a new hobby

Alternatively, you can distil all the time you used to spend running into an entirely new hobby. Maybe learn a musical instrument or a new language.

Remember it's OK to not be OK

You might feel sad some days but make sure you don't feel sad about feeling sad. You've lost your favourite hobby, one that brought lots of emotional benefits. Of course you won't be happy-clappy every day.

See friends and family

If you were running a lot prior to the injury, you might find that you lost touch with people a bit. Now is a great time to reconnect with them, before your injury clears up and you disappear again in a puff of running smoke.

Through puddles

A BIT OF FUN

After all that talk of health and safety, it's time to remind ourselves that running is actually great fun. So here, the *Code* will tell you how to splash through puddles, why it's important to check yourself out in shop windows, and why a big run on the horizon doesn't mean you have to cut back on frolicks in the bedroom.

We also touch on the hilarious horror of official race photos, learn how to crowbar into every conversation the fascinating news that we have run a marathon and then we tackle the big one: fart etiquette for runners.

We'll even find time to have a good rant about the enemy of every true runner: the treadmill. All in all, it's going to be quite a ride – so strap in and enjoy.

THE GOOD, THE BAD AND THE UGLY

Splash through puddles

If you are running in the park and you see a big puddle in the distance, sometimes it can be tempting to splash your way through it. You can feel in touch with nature as you kick the water up in the air. It is also empowering: rather than worrying about your feet getting wet, you are insisting that your feet get soaked. Plus, it's great fun. As long as you're not going to get anyone else wet, then fill your boots!

GUEST FEATURE | *Louise Minchin*

A thing I love about running: I love the frisson of shock and energy that shoots through me when my feet splash into the first puddle on a cold, wet, muddy run, and knowing, as the filthy water soaks through my socks and shoes, that the worst moment of my day is over, and things are only going to get better.

A thing I hate about running: I hate seeing other runners when I am injured and unable to run. Every time I catch sight of someone running, whether they are on a gentle jog or bouncing along at speed I feel a surge of irrational, overwhelming running envy.

Louise Minchin is a distinguished BBC broadcaster and the author of Dare to Tri: My Journey from the BBC Breakfast Sofa to Team GB Triathlete.

Avoid treadmills

Do you find running on a treadmill a tiresome and unrewarding experience? Of course you do. Running in the gym is really, really boring. Without fresh air and constantly changing scenery, running quickly becomes tiresome. There is nothing to look at apart from grimacing, grunting men, slightly uncomfortable women or the ticker-tape depression of rolling news channels. Rather than delighting in the sounds of nature, you have the sounds of grunting weightlifters and self-satisfied personal trainers. It's all far from ideal.

They really are beastly machines. Treadmills transform even the fittest and most accomplished of outdoor runners into wheezing resisters within minutes of starting to run on their silly belts. That distance number on the screen just won't move forwards. Every metre feels like a kilometre. My god, I hate them.

Put simply, running on a treadmill is boring and torturous. There is a good reason for that: it was originally designed for English prisons as a tool for punishment. Among the first inmates to endure the punishment was Oscar Wilde.

Within minutes of starting you begin to wonder whether anti-terror detectives should use treadmills to help break down suspects. Just tell them to run even 8km (5 miles) on one and surely before the first kilometre was finished, they would break down and confess to every act of terror that has ever been committed since the dawn of time.

Despite my rant, however, there are times when running on a treadmill is acceptable. If the roads outside are too icy or snowy to run safely on then a trot in the gym is a good idea. If you can't sleep in a hotel then nipping down to their gym in the wee hours is probably safer than running around an unfamiliar metropolis. During recovery from certain injuries, too, a treadmill can be helpful.

Or, if you find yourself in outer space, a treadmill is probably your most straightforward option. The British astronaut Tim Peake ran the London Marathon from space in April 2016 on a treadmill and completed the distance in 3 hours, 35 minutes and 21 seconds.

But outside of those exceptions, it's never really running if you are doing it on a treadmill. What's more, a study found that those who run in the open air show higher post-workout self-esteem than those who work out in the gym. So get out of the gym and on to the road. You're a harrier not a hamster.

For the sake of completeness, assuming that you need to run on one for a while, here is your survival guide to easing the boredom:

- Change an aspect of the experience every 400m (0.25 miles). You can change the incline or the speed, for instance. Or skip to a different song if you've got your headphones in.
- Another way to stave off the yawns can be to catch up on your podcasts or engross yourself in a fascinating audiobook.
- Break your run up with another form of exercise: so if you have a 16km (10-mile) target you could run 9.6km (6 miles) and then go and do some work on the rowing machine or a cross-trainer, before returning to the treadmill.

I hope these help, though in my opinion you really should try to boycott treadmills. Maybe if enough people were to do this, treadmills would eventually give up and return to the depths of hell whence they emerged.

You can never own too many running books

It's a little-known (but definitely true) fact that owning lots of running books gives you the edge as a runner. In fact, I've heard that buying multiple copies of the same running book could make you a world champion. Finally, if a running book has made you chuckle, it can be an act of great charity to buy copies of it for everyone you know. Just thought I'd mention it.

Downplay what others think is extraordinary

When you arrive at the office in the morning and inform your colleagues that you've already run 16km (10 miles) before work, they might be amazed. When you tell people you've run three marathons, they might think this is extraordinary. The trick is to play it down with a dismissive shrug because then you look even more heroic and superior to them. It's important to really rub it in.

Check yourself out in shop windows

If you put a lot of time, effort and dedication into anything then it's natural to wonder if you're getting the benefits. It's true that many of us who run mostly do so for the emotional rather than physical benefits. We are more interested in a healthy mind than a sexy body ... but that doesn't mean we're not up for getting our body a bit peachier if we can manage it!

So, by all means do check yourself out as you pass shop windows. Probably best not to do it in house windows, though. While shopworkers are likely to be amused at worst by a passing narcissist, for those minding their own business in their living rooms it might be a bit much to suddenly see a stranger checking out their own backside.

Learn to love runners' small talk

Forget what you've heard about people showing up to parkruns to run. Many parkrunners are actually just there to chat, so plan on having to engage in quite a lot of it, unless you don't mind appearing rude. Topics you'll be expected to converse about include:

Your plans for the parkrun

Are you planning to 'give it some' or 'take it easy' for instance? It doesn't seem acceptable to not have a plan but it does seem fine to lie, because moments before the starting pistol, many a parkrunner has declared that they are going to 'take it easy' before setting off at sprinting pace and smashing their PB.

Any injuries you have

Don't think people will be bored or repulsed by the finer details of your tight hamstring or your plantar fasciitis. The more details the better. Do you have a slight 'niggle' in your right knee but are hoping the morning's trot will 'run it off'? This is mind-bending, tell as many people as you can!

The weather

What is the weather like? What did you expect the weather to be like? Had you heard it was going to be raining, even though it isn't? Make sure you share this meteorological gold with your fellow runners.

Talk it through

At the finishing line, be sure to dissect your run in astonishing detail. Perhaps you found it a challenge but are glad you did it, at the end of the day? Did you find that you set out a bit too fast and then 'really paid for it' in the final third? Well, tell people, then!

Share your time

Although you timed your run on your watch, do you suspect that actually you stopped the timer a few seconds late, and therefore your actual finish time might be two or three seconds faster than your watch is telling you? It would be selfish to keep this intrigue to yourself!

Silence is golden

The only time you are not usually expected to chat is during the run itself. I say 'not usually' because you will occasionally find a parkrunner who will sidle up to you during the run and try to chat there. Even though you are both out of breath. The best answer to this is to ask them something about themselves and let them do the talking, while you preserve your oxygen for the run. Or run away from them. Fast.

Don't get your hopes up for race photos

The camera never lies, they say. Well, whoever coined that term clearly wasn't a runner because we know that the camera does lie. It lies so very much. In fact, it lies so much it makes Donald Trump seem like a beacon of truth.

Parkrun photographs are the most regular offenders for the disappointing race photo. Oftentimes, the parkrun photographer is a volunteer, kindly giving up their morning to snap with a camera phone. They don't claim to be David Bailey and boy are they absolutely right to not claim to be David Bailey.

As you run in the third kilometre, you notice the parkrun photographer ahead. You wipe your face and improve your posture for the impending snap. You might even speed up or slow down a bit to move out from the crowd, so the snapper can take a nice clear picture of you in all your athletic glory.

Later, as the photos are uploaded online, you search through them for your moment of pictorial glory. Before you even find your photo, you can just imagine the floods of 'likes' it will attract when you set it as your profile photo on Facebook.

But then you find it and rather than a crisp image of you looking like some sort of striding pin-up, you find a blurry picture of you like some sort of wounded yeti. Your posture is twisted, your face is exhausted and snot is flying out of your beak. The photo is more likely to attract pity rather than the envy we hope our social media images will spark. (Yes, envy. Please don't pretend you don't know what I mean.)

All of these problems are only magnified at bigger running events. At many half marathons and marathons there are professional photographers who snap away and then upload the photographs on to a server. Runners can then search using their race number for the watermarked images of themselves that they can buy.

We are so excited when we get the email notifying us that our photographs are ready for our perusal. Instagram glory is just moments away! But all too often we don't want to buy them because the sharper lenses and finer eyes of the professional photographer only magnify what the parkrun amateur was hinting at. The wrinkles, the weird posture and even the very saliva on our chins is all there, in unforgiving, high-definition glory. You might be running forwards but your face is going off in all directions. The top half is contorted to the right, the bottom half is slanting out to the left. It's as if your face is trying to snap itself in half. And rather than appearing to effortlessly glide, you look like you're running your 800th kilometre (500th mile) through treacle. Often, you'll be grimacing as if you're breaking wind, or worse. Basically, the absolute *state* of you!

Far from wanting to pay the photographer for the chance to download your race photograph, you want to pay them to destroy the photos and make sure no human being ever sees them. The only way to avoid this disappointment is not to get your hopes up in the first place. Assume the official race photos will be awful and ask a loved one to take a picture of you afterwards, with your medal.

Learn to recognise other runners in their civvies

Running is not a team game and for some of us, this is why we enjoy it. But all the same, a bit of running solidarity can be a good thing. It's easy to recognise a runner while they are running. They'll be the ones in sporty clothes, moving very fast down a road or path. But how do you recognise another runner in more everyday scenarios? It's easy when you know what you're looking for...

- They might well have a very prominent Adam's apple (if they're a man).
- They stretch all the time: in the queue at the supermarket, during a drinks party, while watching a rock concert, as they exchange vows at a wedding, while being vaccinated for Covid-19...
- They crowbar into every conversation that they've run a marathon.
- They wear running shoes with non-running clothes, including suits.
- They have tan lines all year round.
- They carry bananas around with them.
- They carefully measure out the carbs on their plate.
- They wear a sports watch all the time.
- Whenever you see them at the shops, they are buying bagels.

Fart etiquette

This is an awkward topic but one that must be tackled. Healthy food makes you healthier, clearly, but the horrid truth is that healthy food also makes you windier. Spoon into this heady mix the fact that a lot of us get a bit nervous about running and then consider that running makes your gastrointestinal tract bounce around, and you have a perfect storm. A perfect storm of wind.

Well, that storm only gets windier when you consider that aerobic exercise accelerates the process of breaking down food, which results in the faster production of hydrogen, carbon dioxide and methane. And there's more: understand that as we run we often contract our core muscles and colons, which also helps more wind get squeezed out. These are uncomfortable truths, but truths all the same.

It's no use burying your head in the sand, you have to face this problem head on. So here is your guide to fart etiquette during runs. Or, your gas guidelines, if you will.

- If you are running more than 24km (15 miles), never risk a suspicious fart. Nike's slogan may be 'Just Do It' but when it comes to potentially wet farts, the very opposite is true.
- If you are a man and running with a group of male runners, feel free not only to fart but also to greet it with a laddish 'Wahey!' If your fellow runners have anything about them at all, they will high five you.
- Apologise quickly if any fellow runners took offence. The awkward moment will pass quicker.
- Feel free to fart to entertain yourself during long solo runs. In fact, you must do so.
- Don't fart into the path of someone running directly behind you. If you've got to let rip, then let do it to the side of the path, or at the back of the pack.
- That said, you could do it tactically. When the urge to fart strikes, make your way to the very front of the pack (while carefully retaining your nascent gust) and then let it go. With any luck, your fellow runners will be so appalled they will slow down to avoid the absolute hell you left behind in your wake.

- If someone else farts, try to respond compassionately. This means not drawing attention to it unless they do.
- If you don't want people to notice your fart, you could try coughing loudly as you let it out, to drown out the noise. Or, you can wait for a passing car or other noisy occurrence and try to slip one out subtly then.
- If you don't want to fart, decrease your portions of windy foods such as beans and other vegetables, especially in the meals you eat ahead of a run. If you have particularly bad problems with wind then consider trying charcoal tablets. The charcoal absorbs gas in the digestive system, which helps reduce symptoms. But really, as a runner you are never going to entirely avoid farting, so it is best to stop worrying and learn to love it. Follow the *Code* and you won't go far wrong.

Don't let someone in a costume beat you

It's not going to do your self-esteem much good to be overtaken by someone dressed as an elephant or the Eiffel Tower. So outrun them wherever they appear or you might regret it for the rest of your life.

Don't go chaste on us

Athletes can be an easily aroused bunch: at the Olympic village, as many as 42 condoms are factored in for each athlete. Honestly, you saucy sods!

Yet you don't need to be in the running for a gold medal to be a horny harrier. Even the more everyday runner stands a strong chance of being a bit more randy than most. For instance, there is a 30 per cent reduction in the risk of erectile dysfunction among men who run vigorously more than once a week, according to the *Annals of Internal Medicine*.

For women, running can help strengthen hips, boosting performance between the sheets. A study for the University of Arkansas found that 80 per cent of men and 60 per cent of women felt more attractive due to regular running. It makes you feel good in your body, which boosts sexual confidence.

Running also promotes circulation and blood flow to all parts of the body. *All* parts of the body. Plus, all that dopamine that you produce by running boosts arousal. It's a wonder we ever get out of bed long enough to run.

Sometimes, people ask runners whether they have to be chaste the night before a running event. Yet talk of people being ordered to abstain from sex the night before a big event is a bit of a myth. Many experts say there's nothing wrong with a spot of nooky the night before – as long as it doesn't come after long nights trawling bars and clubs in search of it. And we can also file this issue away under the heading: get over yourself, you're not running in the Olympics.

It's worth bearing in mind, though, that too much running is likely to harm your sex life. Excessive weekly mileage is going to truly exhaust you and possibly destroy your sex drive.

So, get the balance right and you can enjoy enhanced experiences of both of the pastimes that make you sweat.

Learn to always mention you've run a marathon

Question: How do you know when someone's run a marathon?

Answer: They'll tell you.

We've all heard that joke. It points to the cliché that people who have run a marathon are always telling people that they've run a marathon. It may or may not be true but it's what everyone assumes.

Well, this sets up a conundrum. If everyone assumes that marathon runners always tell people that they've run a marathon, this means that unless you tell people about the marathon that you've run, they will assume you *haven't* run a marathon – and that won't do at all!

So here are some handy tips to, ever so smoothly and seamlessly, work into conversation that you've run a marathon:

- When someone mentions something that is long, say: 'Oh, a bit like a marathon, then? I've run a marathon!'
- On the 26th day of any month, ask people what the date is. When they tell you, reply: 'Oh, 26 – the same number of miles as in a marathon... I ran a marathon once!'
- When someone describes anything as 'gruelling,' say: 'A bit like a marathon... I ran a marathon once!'
- If someone pays you any compliment on your appearance, say: 'Oh, it must be that marathon I once ran!'
- On any Monday, ask someone what day of the week it is. When they tell you, reply: 'Oh, Monday – a word that begins with an 'm', like 'marathon'... I ran a marathon once!'
- If someone is eating a Snickers bar, remind them that Snickers used to be called Marathon. You know what to do next.

With any luck, at this stage the other person will ask you what it's like to run a marathon. You've hit the jackpot: they've given you the green light to tell them all about it. Tell them about the training, the run itself and how you felt afterwards. Scroll through your phone and find that photo of you with your medal.

Ideally, when you tell people about the marathon you've run, you should strive for a balance between describing it as both a difficult and easy challenge. 'Yes, it is very, very hard to run a marathon,' you tell them, 'but I actually found it quite easy.' Really lay it on thick.

Once you've exhausted everything you want to say about your marathon, it's time to give them a chance to speak. So say: 'Anyway, enough about my marathon, what do you think about my marathon?'

GUEST FEATURE | *Liz Yelling*

A thing I love about running: I love the freedom running gives me, I can go anywhere my fitness will allow, and it means I get to see places on foot that not everyone can see. I love the clearness and the clarity that running gives my mind and the feeling of peace with my inner self that I have when I get back from a run. Running for me helps me make sense of the world, running away anxieties and balls of frustration helps me enjoy my week with more calm. I am not really 'me' without some running in my week.

> **The thing I hate about running:** That it can be a reflection of your inner self ... when all I want is for my running to be effortless. If I run when I am super stressed, slightly ill or hormonally unbalanced, I crawl ... each step is an effort and all I want is that metronomic effortless shuffle. However, running actually helps, even if it can feel bad sometimes.
>
> *Liz is a two-time Olympic marathon runner and Commonwealth medallist British long-distance runner.*

Don't use running as an excuse

Sometimes people – well, I say 'people' but we're mostly talking men – use their hobbies to get out of domestic responsibilities. This is definitely not OK and using running for that purpose is not OK either.

Weekends are the core battleground for this domestic culture war. Saturday mornings have become a popular time for running. Your weekend is just starting up, so after all the hassle of your working week, it feels great to get out there and run free. Parkrun and many other running events are held on Saturday mornings and a lot of running clubs assemble then, too. It is the happy hour of harriers, so it's lovely to get out there and drink it all in.

But wait a moment: the problem is that a lot of other things happen on Saturday mornings, too. For parents of school-age children, Saturday mornings can often become their unofficial chauffeur shift. With music classes, groups, birthday parties and other activities, it falls to parents to shuttle their kids to and from it all. Also, a lot of people like to do their main supermarket shop of the week on a Saturday morning.

So if there is one runner in a marriage, they can easily cause tension and resentment if they fly out of the door every Saturday morning, leaving their partner to deal with all the tasks. Indeed, this can be just as inflammatory if both partners are runners, and one of them pulls rank to go off for a run. I've often heard a man brag at parkrun that he convinced 'the missus' to stay home with the kids so he could go running. Classy.

It isn't just that it's unfair and unwise for you to do this, the simple truth is that if you start running for the wrong reasons, running won't reward you in the same way. The purity of running is one of its big joys and you shouldn't compromise that by using it for nefarious means.

Running is an honest hobby and you must approach it with honesty. This is the Instagram era, when people constantly pretend to be something they're not. People have us believe they are richer, more successful and happier than they are. Among all this hot air, there's something wonderful about the truthfulness of running. You only get out of running what you put into it. So let's keep it pure and lovely, right?

The *Code* is absolutely serious about this: *don't* use running as an excuse.

But also, *do* use running as an excuse!

Actually, it doesn't pay to be too saintly about running. There are many ways you can use running to get out of things. If you're training for a marathon, for instance, you'll find this can be a great get-out clause for social events you either want to leave early or avoid altogether.

The boss has suggested a Friday night work drinking session and you're worried you'll get cornered by that bore from human resources. The solution? Turn up for a half-pint and when you've finished nursing it for 30 minutes, announce that you've got a long training run in the morning and you have to leave. Invited to a Saturday night party you really don't fancy? Tell them that Sunday morning is your long-run day and you really can't be staying out late on a Saturday night.

The Christmas period is when all this comes into its own. The festive season is one of office parties, family get-togethers and other social horrors that many people are desperate to get out of. It all climaxes with the enforced 'fun' of New Year's Eve and its inane countdown at 11.59 p.m. Want to get out of it? Just play the running card.

This can also be used to escape the cabin fever of long family gatherings over Christmas itself. Those epic, rolling affairs in which several wings and generations of a clan are gathered together in a house, which is all Christmas jumpers and Brussels sprouts flatulence. How to escape the claustrophobia? If you say you're going for a walk, you raise the risk of some bore saying they'll join you. You haven't escaped the problem, you've just moved it to a different place.

So, your best bet is to say you're going for a run. There is still the chance of some bore wanting to join you, but it is most likely that you'll get to escape the lot of them. The best way to introduce the idea is to wait until someone worries out loud about how many calories they have consumed during Christmas. You can always rely on someone to trot out this knackered old cliché. Once they do, just announce: 'And on that note, I must take your leave for a while and burn off some of my calories!'

Now you can get into your running gear and speed off to the freedom and relief of the open road. If you really need a prolonged break, do the longest run you can manage and then extend your liberty even longer by loitering for a while in a park or pub. Play your cards right and you can have several hours of freedom out there. The bliss of it!

All jokes aside, perhaps the real message here is one of balance. Don't use running as an excuse to get out of things you really ought to be doing: domestic responsibilities such as childcare or shopping. But equally, definitely do use running as an excuse to get out of horrors that have been unfairly inflicted upon you.

Don't run on the beach

The late polemicist Christopher Hitchens famously said: 'The four most overrated things in life are champagne, lobster, anal sex and picnics.' Runners could add to that list: running on the beach.

In your mind, running on a beach seems absolutely idyllic. But in the real world? Not so much. For a start, it's a grind. Sand is harder to run on: it requires 1.6 times as much energy expenditure as running on a firmer surface. A 2013 study published in the *Journal of Strength and Conditioning Research* found that running on sand forces your body to work at least 10 per cent harder than it does on grass.

The uneven surface also increases the chances of several injuries, including a sprained ankle or tendinopathy. Your hip- and knee-stabilising muscles are working nearly twice as hard, according to a study published in the *European Journal of Applied Physiology*. This means your heart rate and blood lactate threshold are raised. Basically, running on the slope towards the sea itself can create all sorts of injury woes.

And anyway, it's so clichéd to run on a beach. In drama, if they want a heroic character to go for a morning or sunset run, they love it to take place on the beach. Well, it's fine for the movies. In real life, running on the beach is a vastly overrated thing.

IT'S ALL IN THE HEAD

Modern sport is as much about mind games as ball games. From baseball bosses trying to freak out their rivals to coaches employing sports psychologists to bend the minds of their players, it seems that it's not just football that thinks head games are important.

For runners, the mind can be used to make running more enjoyable and successful. From listening to your inner monologue to listening to music, to visualisation, mindfulness and dealing with anxiety, there are many mental improvements we can make.

LISTEN UP

You might think that running is all about your legs but your ears can play a big part, too. If you listen to your body you can avoid burning out. If you need a distraction during a long run, music or audiobooks can be your best friend. We're getting nearer the finishing line but there's still some learning to be done.

Listen to your body

Why, as a runner, should you listen to your body and not your mind? To put it simply: your mind often lies but your body always tells the truth. If you don't believe me, see if either of these scenarios ring any bells with you:

1. You know you really should be doing a long run this coming weekend but part of you doesn't fancy it. Suddenly, your mind sets to work and conjures up a conveyor belt of reasons why you shouldn't be running this weekend. You need to clear out the garage. You need to spend more time with your partner. You are sure you felt a nasty twinge in your calf and if you don't rest, it might develop into something more serious.

2. You actually did have a nasty twinge in your calf and it actually did develop into something more serious. Now, your body is clearly telling you it is time to rest. The very last thing you should be doing is getting out there for a run. Again, your mind comes up with it's own commentary. Well, a little run wouldn't hurt, would it? It might actually make the injury better. Didn't you read something online once about how you can 'run off' any injury? Sounds good, right?

In both scenarios, your body is a reliable and trustworthy commentator – and both times, your mind is lying to you.

Taking a rest when your body tells you to is not a sign of weakness, but is actually a signal that you have the willingness and intelligence to recognise your true physical limits, rather than the limits you wish you have. A runner who ignores the physical signs that they are injured will most likely suffer a longer downtime as their injury, now more grave, slowly heals.

An effective way to learn to listen to your body is to keep a training log and note down any issues, however minor, you felt during your run. If on a Monday you have a bit of discomfort in your left foot, that might be useful to remember when, the following week, your right foot packs up completely. This will teach you how to spot the signs and demonstrates why it's important to listen to them.

The flipside of listening to your body is not listening so much to your mind. If your body is fine to run, don't let your mind convince you that there's a problem that isn't there.

It's just a question of listening. Once you start, you will find that your body provides you with constant feedback that can help improve your running performance.

Also, listen to music

Run Society says listening to music can boost your running performance by up to 15 per cent. Here's how.

Build a 'cheesy running songs' playlist

Go on, you know you want to. Here are some suggestions:

- 'Start Me Up' – The Rolling Stones
- 'Stronger' – Kanye West

- 'Eye of the Tiger' – Survivor
- 'All The Small Things' – blink-182
- 'Jump' (2015 Remaster) – Van Halen
- 'The Best' – Tina Turner
- 'Keep on Running' – Spencer Davis Group
- 'Work Bitch' – Britney Spears
- 'Banjo Hill' – The Cropdusters
- 'Paradise City' – Guns N' Roses
- 'Are You Gonna Go My Way' – Lenny Kravitz
- 'Happy' – Pharrell Williams
- 'Harder Better Faster' – Daft Punk

The rule of audiobooks

However much you pay attention to that nine-hour audiobook you listen to on runs, you will keep zoning out and then having to rewind and starting again from chapter one. You never find out who did the murder but you can recite the first chapter off by heart.

Let your imagination run wild

Even if you love listening to music or chat as you run, it is worth occasionally leaving the headphones at home and experiencing a run with just the soundtrack of the world and your mind's own rich imagination.

Ignore warnings from non-runners

There are many running experts out there. From coaches, to physios, to retired professionals and even your humble authors of running books, it seems a lot of people know a lot about running. But it turns out that actually, we know nothing.

Because the people who know most about running are people who have never run a mile in their lives. You heard that right – the true running expert is the person who never runs and who doesn't want to run. The moment they learn that you are a runner, these people will happily fill you in with their athletic wisdom.

Most runners have been in this situation. You mention that you like running and suddenly someone pipes up with a monologue of apocalyptic warnings about how exercise is the most dangerous thing ever. It's quite a hill to die on but they are more than happy to die on it. (As long as someone drives them uphill because they sure won't be running up no slopes.)

They are always particularly concerned about one part of your body. 'Ooh, I've heard that running is terrible for knees,' they say, with a wince. It's a curious thing: they have never previously mentioned having decades of experience in osteopathy. They have kept hidden the PhD certificates and other medical qualifications they must have, to be such knee experts.

And not just knee experts – but knee-botherers, too. They stare at your knees as one might regard a wounded animal, or a baby about to crawl off the side of a cliff. It's as if they're considering having you put down, such is the obvious danger you are putting your knees in.

Don't bother telling them that your knees feel fine because what the hell would you know? It's not worth pointing out that, according to a Boston University study, regular running actually improves knee health by strengthening bones and joints – because their confidence trumps anyone's objective expertise.

There is plenty more you can throw at them, though. In 2016, the *Journal of the American Medical Association* found that high-fitness exercisers, including runners, had a lower risk for developing 26 different kinds of cancer than low- and non-exercisers. Running can also improve cognitive function, and reduce cognitive decline and Alzheimer's disease. Humans create fewer brain cells as we age but a study at the University of Cambridge found that regular running can reverse this development. Running boosts your memory by stimulating brain growth, particularly in the hippocampus region. A one-hour run adds seven hours to your life, according to research for *Progress in Cardiovascular Diseases*.

And yet all of that will fall on deaf ears because the one thing that every couch potato knows for sure is that running destroys knees. They don't know how or why they know it, they just know it. Even as all human history shows that we were given legs to run with, they stand against it. There's a lot of these people around.

Likewise, every runner's family should include one relative who will stare worriedly into the face of every runner and tell them that they look thin and tired. Now, it's true that having a lean body and taking in lots of sun while you are out and about can lead to a gaunt look to your face. But you have to consider what this relative is really bothered by: it's your fit body. When they tell you that you look too thin, they mean you look too thin in comparison to their flabby folds. What they're really saying is: I want a thin face and you've got a thin face and I want your thin face, too!

The bottom line is that running looks like hard work and it does involve hard work. Even though that hard work brings with it no end of benefits, such as health, happiness and fun, the hard work part of running scares people. And because people don't like admitting that they're scared of hard work, they have to come up with other reasons and excuses for not doing it. 'Well, I'd love to run but it's so bad for the knees' is a useful cop-out.

So don't worry about it. They're not really arguing with you, they are arguing with their own excuses, bickering with their own consciences. Other types of people face similar nonsense. If you tell people that you are teetotal or vegan, you will face a similar barrage of defence mechanisms. Veganism and non-drinking seem to unsettle some people's consciences in the same way running does. (As a vegan, non-drinking runner, I should know.)

So, although it is important to avoid injuries and to take care of your body, don't listen to these people who make wild claims about your knees. They know not what they speak of and their concern is for their own wheezy consciences, not you.

Another line they like to trot out is that running is antisocial and only for misanthropes. If you hear this one, you can just smile politely and reflect on the fact that people who say things like this are enough to make anyone a misanthrope who wants to escape humanity. So just smile and wait for them to get tired and waddle off. Or take matters into your own hands. Put on your running shoes and run away from them. Ahhh, that's feeling better already, isn't it?

TRICKS OF THE MIND

Mental tricks to keep yourself buoyant can be as beneficial as any physical trick. For most runners, your body can run much further than your mind sometimes believes it can. So try different mental games to make sure you are the best runner you can be.

Run in the moment

Runners can learn a lot from those in abstinence-based recovery groups. In Alcoholics Anonymous they drill into people that they should take things one day at a time. Projecting forward is likely to overwhelm those recovering from addiction but if they vow to not return to drinking in a particular day, then that feels possible. The same approach can work wonders for runners.

If you feel tired in mile 7 of a half marathon, the thought of running 6 miles more is overwhelming. So the trick is not to think about miles 8, 9, 10, 11, 12 or 13. Instead, just think about mile 7. Think about the mile you are currently running. Then, when you've run that one, think about the next one.

Clearly, though, you must on some level be at least a little mindful of the full distance you are running. You mustn't approach mile 7 of a half marathon as the final mile of the run. A sprint finish at that stage would be counter-productive and would look really weird.

Break it down

A related mental tactic to staying in the moment is to make a switch midway through the distance. In the second half of the run, count how many miles you have left, rather than how many you have run. So if we take the half marathon example again, after mile 9 you will not be thinking 'nine' but 'four' – as that is how many miles you have left. The theory goes that thinking of a smaller, rather than a larger number, will give you a boost.

Another method some runners use is to break down a long run into smaller increments. For instance, marathon runners will break the 42.2km (26.2 miles) into groups of 3.2km (2 miles) in their heads. They run 3.2km (2 miles), then they run 3.2km (2 miles), then they run 3.2km (2 miles) more. Eventually, after 13 groups of just 3.2km (2 miles) at a time, they have run a marathon. It sounds easy when you put it like that, right?

Be mindful

Mindfulness has risen in popularity at around the same time as the boom in running's popularity. Naturally, the two trends have combined into one: mindful running. In essence, running is about being mentally connected within your movement and not being distracted. Many mindful runners like to focus on their breath: what does their breath tell them about their body?

There are many apps, training programmes and even books that can guide the runner into the delicious world of mindful running. Many who test this path find that the more connected to their running they become, the further and longer they can run. Namaste!

GUEST FEATURE | *Cindy Kuzma*

A thing I love about running: One thing I love about running is the way it offers a chance to test body and mind, to see what we're made of when times get tough. It's a hard thing I do voluntarily, so I know that when I face challenges beyond my control, I can rise to meet them.

In the middle of a hard workout or a long race, I often wonder if I can go on. Most times, I do, and find that I'm stronger than I thought. In other tough moments, I stop or slow down. Then, too, I learn something – that failure won't destroy me, my support team still stands by me, and I can lace up and try again.

A thing I hate about running: One thing I hate about running is its high-impact nature – if it weren't so hard on my body, I wouldn't have developed so many injuries. It can feel devastating to invest so much into something and then have it taken away from you, even temporarily.

That said, each setback has taught me something important about myself. Even the heartbreak has been invaluable. So many of the runners and other athletes in our book *Rebound* felt the same. They hated the experience of being injured and wouldn't wish the pain on anyone, but nearly every single one said that if they had it all to do again, they wouldn't change anything because of the person they became on the other side.

Cindy is the co-host of The Injured Athletes Club *podcast and co-author of* Rebound: Train Your Mind to Bound Back Stronger from Sports Injuries.

Embrace pre-run anxiety

After spending months preparing for a running event, you'd think you'd wake up feeling happy on the big day. However, for many runners, they wake up feeling miserable and anxious. This can range from anything like mild discomfort and worry to full-blown panic, with all the nausea and repetitive toilet visits that entails.

Quickly, this pre-run terror can start to feed itself. As you worry about the race, you begin to worry that your worry will drain your energy and make the race harder. And that makes you worry even more about the race, and so on.

There are ways to reduce anxiety but another approach is not to fight it but to embrace it. See it as a sign of how much your run means to you. If you woke up indifferent on the day then what would have been the point of the whole thing? I find that the more anxious I am about a race beforehand, the better I feel afterwards.

Also, remember that pre-run nerves will nearly always disappear within minutes of the start. So when you arrive at the race, just focus on your warm-up, safe in the knowledge that you'll feel fine soon.

Cherish your running-related anxiety dreams

Running-related anxiety dreams can come in many shapes and sizes. You may dream that you are taking part in an important event but for some reason you've forgotten how to run. Your legs just won't move. (In the real world, you'll probably be kicking the mattress at this point as you try desperately to get your legs to run.)

In another common scenario, you find yourself late for an important running event, and the realisation begins to dawn on you that you are going to miss it. All that preparation you put in and now you're going to miss out!

Well, experts say that if you are dreaming about something going wrong, it is a sign that the thing is important to you. So take these anxiety dreams as signs that you've found a hobby that is important to you and that you are taking it seriously. So that's a positive. And remember: it really was just a dream.

React well to a bad performance

Sometimes, you will have a bad day in your running shoes. A training run will be more of a strain than you could ever have imagined. Your dream of a sub-20 minute parkrun will go completely wrong, leaving you panting over the line in 26 minutes. Or, on a longer distance, your body will pack up and you won't finish the distance.

After a good run, it's lovely to return home. You come back through the front door with the physical and emotional glow of a successful, enjoyable run. Your body and mind feel great. But after a bad run, it's the opposite. Every sinew of your body, and all of your mind, feel sad and broken.

There's nothing you can do to change the past, so what matters at this stage is what you do next. The poet John Keats described failure as the 'highway to success'. Certainly, once you learn to embrace failure, you can only improve.

The wise runner will take any failure or setback as a golden opportunity to analyse information, learn and improve. Try to pinpoint what went wrong and why. Ask yourself tough questions and answer them truthfully. Had you prepared properly for the run? Or had you cut corners with your training?

Also, at this stage it is good to accept that sometimes a bad run can be just down to a stroke of bad luck and is therefore nothing to get your running shorts in a twist about.

Then move forwards: if you were disappointed by your performance at an event, book in for another event, a sensible distance into the future. Joining a half marathon the following weekend only risks doubling your disappointment, but one several months into the future gives you a nice target to aim at.

While it's important to address what you can control, you should also make sure you let go of what you cannot control. Follow the serenity prayer. This prayer is popular in abstinence-based recovery groups and is also a fine guidance for the disappointed runner. It goes: 'God, grant me the serenity to accept the things I cannot change, courage to change the things I can, and wisdom to know the difference.'

None of this is meant to dismiss the feelings of disappointment after a bad run. If running is your passion and it goes wrong for you, it is natural to feel sad. Express how you feel and let your passion show. Analyse what went wrong and how you can use it to improve. And then set about learning how to come back stronger.

GUEST FEATURE *Nita Sweeney*

A thing I love about running:

Running is alchemical. I leave the house struggling to remember how to tie my shoes and come home ready to try out for the Olympic marathon. But some days, the reverse is also true. I leave the house excited for a hard workout and come home shredded, but still transformed.

On a given day, running shows me who I am that day. Tired or energised. Willing or reluctant. Running shows that to me. Over a period of time, it shows who I've become. I didn't think I could finish a book and get it published. I tried. Depression and anxiety blocked my efforts. Until I built stamina from long-distance training, I wasn't able to complete a project. Until running transformed my mood, I struggled to face the work. Now I have two books published and am working on a third. Running gave me that and so much more. It gave me my life back.

A thing I hate about running:

It's hard to think of something I hate about running since it has brought me so many benefits. But I do struggle with accepting my pace. I was slow when I began to run. I'm not happy about that and even less happy about how much slower I get as I age. But that's not running's fault. Running doesn't judge. It's here for me no matter how old or slow I get.

Nita Sweeney is the award-winning author of Depression Hates a Moving Target: How Running with My Dog Brought Me Back from the Brink.

TAKE IN YOUR SURROUNDINGS

I don't know about you but sometimes when I finish a run, I find the whole thing went by in a blur. Perhaps I was thinking something over. Or, I was gripped by a podcast. I can sometimes come back from a 16km (10-mile) run and hardly have a memory of where I ran or what sights there were on the route.

This is a shame because taking in the sights during a long run can be one of its most simple joys. If I am on a new route, or running in a new area, there will be new things to feast my eyes upon. Even if I am running on a familiar path, there are the changes of the seasons to observe. The birds coming and going, the leaves growing and then falling. The furry creatures going into and emerging from hibernation.

In truth, I sometimes miss this because I'm so mentally absorbed that I just keep my eyes slanted downwards and my attention directed inwards. Mindfulness coaches encourage people to get into the moment by naming something they can see, hear and smell.

You can follow a similar approach as you run. It can be great to regularly ask yourself: what can I see, hear and smell? It brings you right into the moment and restores your awareness of what is around you.

If you dismiss the benefits of being aware during a run as woo-woo concepts of mindfulness and being in the moment, then remember that on a practical level they are also about safety. If you're keeping your eyes open and your wits about you then you are less likely to come to any harm by tripping over or being mugged. It's amazing how many hidden tree roots I have discovered the hard way in my local parks.

Problem-solving in your head is one of the benefits of running but I don't think we should be too internalised every time. So next time you are out on a run, take a look at what's going on around you for a bit.

RUN HAPPY

hope this book has reminded you how wonderful running is but also how deliciously daft it can be.

Although it is mostly a solitary pursuit, running still has an impact on others and we can help make the world a nicer place each time we run. If we follow the *Code* then with each step we can tip the world in a kinder direction.

My closing thought is that there's enough to be serious and grumpy about in life without casting their shadows over your morning run. So remember to run with a smile and enjoy yourself. I bet it will make you go faster.

THE A–Z OF RUNNING

A – Aches
However carefully you follow the *Code* and other wisdom, if you are a runner you will have aches from time to time. Learn to embrace them.

B – Black toenails
If you were to go by the cover models of any running magazine, running is a pastime that makes you beautiful. Simply get a couple of 10Ks under your belt and you'll look gorgeous. What they don't tell you is that running can also give you less desirable features, including spots, chafing and black toenails. I suppose it's understandable that they don't make a big pictorial deal of that.

C – Cool-down
This is an important part of the running process and one that few runners take that seriously. The good news is that this means if you do it well then you are getting ahead of the pack.

D - DNF

The term meaning 'did not finish'. If you have never heard of DNF then well done you!

E - Epsom salts

These are marvellous salts to dissolve in your bath when you have sore muscles or a mild injury. However, do note that these salts are also sometimes used to ease constipation. People mix them with water to get everything moving. I didn't realise this when I first went to a pharmacy to buy some for some muscular problems I was having. When I asked the pharmacist: 'Can I have the biggest tub of Epsom salts you have, please? I've got a major problem to deal with.' I couldn't work out why people in the queue were smirking.

F - Fartlek

And you can stop smirking, too. It just means a form of running that involves varying your pace throughout your run, alternating between fast segments and slow jogs. That said, we've all of us let rip some actual gas once or twice while out running.

G - Gait

Hark at the runners in your local park and their varied gaits. Some stride along gracefully, as if they are the star of a running coaches' video. Others, not so much. Some running gaits are so complex and gnarly that it's more as if they are the star of a horror film.

H - Half marathon

Widely seen as the most middle-of-the-road running distance because it is midway between a marathon and your sofa. I'm a big fan.

I – Ice bath

You know it will do you good but you also know it will hurt. Long-distance runners have something of a love-hate relationship with the ice bath. A quick tip: if you are a man and you are going to have an ice bath, wear shorts. Ice baths can be very unflattering for parts of the male physique. That time I slipped getting out of one and had to call for help was far from ideal for everyone concerned.

K – Kick

The 'kick' is when a runner saves a sprint for the finish of a race. Have you even run a parkrun unless you've at least once suddenly surged forwards in the final 200m (218 yards)?

L – Legs

Runners generally have much nicer legs than non-runners. So there.

M – Marathon

Taking part in a marathon is quite an experience. The emotion of all the runners, the kind, loving support of the spectators, the sheer majesty of the occasion, the bleeding nipples, the people literally shitting themselves in the final few miles...

N – Niggle

This is how runners describe the first hint of an injury. So if you hear a runner talking about a 'niggle' you can usually safely place money on them talking about an 'injury' a week or so later.

O – Out-and-back

The most simple of running routes. You run out in one direction and then turn round and run back in the opposite direction.

It's simple, straightforward and unimaginative. The cheese on brown bread of running routes.

P – Pootle

One of the cuter words to describe a run. If Hugh Grant ever goes out on a run you can guarantee he describes what he just did as a 'pootle'. However, this word is unlikely to catch on widely. I can't imagine people gathering every Saturday for a Parkpootle, having read about it in *Pootlers' World* magazine.

Q – Quicker

What most runners are forever striving to be.

R – Recovery run

The recovery run is a short, gentle run undertaken within 24 hours after a harder run. Some experts say they help facilitate recovery from a long run. Others say they enhance your fitness because you run in a pre-fatigued state, getting more benefit per metre. Either way, they are a good thing to do. And yet even though most runners know this, few actually do them.

S – Stretching

If you ask most runners about stretching, you are likely to get one of two main responses: a great and detailed lecture about the benefits of stretching, or a look of guilt and shame. That just about sums up the approaches of runners to stretching. Some live by it, some never do it.

T – Taper

The part of marathon training when you ramp down your running mileage in the final weeks. You feel both knackered and buzzing with too much energy all at once.

U – Ultra running

What do you do when you've run a marathon? Well, some people pat themselves on the back and return to shorter distances. Others? They look for even longer distances to run. These are ultra runners. They make supermodels look fat and they catch colds a lot.

V – Victory

A lovely thing about running is that you can enjoy personal victories. Unlike being part of a sporting team, or following the fortunes of a sporting team, you are not reliant on others for that sweet moment when you clench your fist and revel in an achievement.

W – Wall

Marathon runners are said to often hit the wall during the final 9.6km (6 miles) of the course but few seem sure whether or not this has happened to them. After all, at that stage of a marathon there is a fine line between hitting the wall and simply being extremely bloody knackered.

Y – Yesterday

Don't worry about what went wrong on your previous run, get thinking about how good you can make your next one.

Z – Zzzz

Nothing beats a good sleep after a long, long run. And because sleeping well makes you run better, you can make this part of your training. Who knew training could be so easy?

ACKNOWLEDGEMENTS

Thank you to everyone at Bloomsbury, especially my wise and compassionate editors, Matt Lowing and Holly Jarrald, and Alice Graham and Katherine Macpherson in marketing and publicity.

Thanks also to Chris Morris, my Mum and Dad, and Lucian Randall, who helped me develop the ideas for this book.

I'm so grateful to my guest contributors who penned their wonderful love/hate entries: Tazneem Anwar, Simon Donnelly, Martin Melly, Louise Minchin, Nicky Campbell, Billy Wingrove, Sean Conway, Henry Winter, Liz Yelling, Claire Maxted, John Brewer, Paul Tonkinson, Paul Hobrough, Lexie Williamson, Martin Yelling, Jonathan Cairns, Anji Andrews, Cindy Kuzma, Michael Stocks, Leanne Davies, Nita Sweeney, Rachel Cullen, Anna McNuff, Tom Usher and Helen Croydon.

Here's mine...

A thing I love about running

I love the 'runners' high'. At school we did cross-country on Wednesday afternoons. If I ran quickly and the buses worked well for me I could get home in time for a triple whammy of soaps: Sons & Daughters, Home & Away and Neighbours. I'd sit there with a sugary tea, my muscles and soul absolutely glowing as I caught up with the averagely acted Aussie drama. Nowadays my post-run favourite is a CBD bath bomb and an audio book but the glow is just the same.

A thing I hate about running

When I'm unable to run due to injury, illness or busyness, I absolutely seethe with resentment if I see anyone else running. Their every step taunts me and convinces me I am on the brink of wheezing obesity. In other words, the only thing I hate about running is not running.

@AllThatChas

Why not share your 'Thing I love/thing I hate about running' on social media, using the hashtag #TheRunnersCode.